Contents

CD contents

Resources and links (MS Word)
Certificate Read-Me (Text file)

Project 1

- Project 1 Completion Certificate (MS Word)
- Project 1 Completion 'Star' Certificate (MS Word)
- Textease examples (t2 files)
- Project 1 Evaluation (MS Word)

Project 2

- Project 2 Completion Certificate (MS Word)
- Project 2 Completion 'Star' Certificate (MS Word)
- Earwig (×2), Snail, and Worm time-lapse movies (AVI files)
- Project 2 Evaluation (MS Word)

Project 3

- Project 3 Completion Certificate (MS Word)
- Project 3 Completion 'Star' Certificate (MS Word)
- 'Cartoon' Textease file (t2 file)
- Project 3 Evaluation (MS Word)

Project 4

- Project 4 Completion Certificate (MS Word)
- Project 4 Completion 'Star' Certificate (MS Word)
- *ReTreeval* handbook (Kudlian Soft) (MS Word)
- Project 4 Evaluation (MS Word)

Project 5

- Project 5 Completion Certificate (MS Word)
- Project 5 Completion 'Star' Certificate (MS Word)

LEARNING ICT with SCIENCE

Other titles in the Teaching ICT through the Primary Curriculum series:

Learning ICT in the Arts
Andrew Hamill
1-84312-313-4

Learning ICT with English
Richard Bennett
1-84312-309-6

Learning ICT in the Humanities
Tony Pickford
1-84312-312-6

Learning ICT with Maths
Richard Bennett
1-84312-310-X

Progression in Primary ICT
Richard Bennett, Andrew Hamill and Tony Pickford
1-84312-308-8

TEACHING ICT ACROSS THE PRIMARY CURRICULUM

LEARNING ICT with SCIENCE

Andrew Hamill

David Fulton Publishers

David Fulton Publishers Ltd
The Chiswick Centre, 414 Chiswick High Road, London W4 5TF

www.fultonpublishers.co.uk
www.onestopeducation.co.uk

First published in Great Britain in 2006 by David Fulton Publishers

10 9 8 7 6 5 4 3 2 1

David Fulton Publishers is a division of Granada Learning Limited, part of ITV plc.

British Library Cataloguing in Publication Data
A catalogue record for this book is available from the British Library.

ISBN: 1-84312-311-8
EAN: 978 1 84312 311 8

Typeset by Servis Filmsetting Ltd, Manchester
Printed and bound in Great Britain

- *Handling Data with Starting Grid/Excel* booklet (MS Word)
- 'Shadow' spreadsheet (MS Excel)
- Textease example (ts file)
- Project 5 Evaluation (MS Word)

Project 6

- Project 6 Completion Certificate (MS Word)
- Project 6 Completion 'Star' Certificate (MS Word)
- 'Giant's hand' spreadsheet (MS Excel)
- Project 6 Evaluation (MS Word)

Project 7

- Project 7 Completion Certificate (MS Word)
- Project 7 Completion 'Star' Certificate (MS Word)
- *Presentations & Interactive Multimedia Packages with PowerPoint* booklet (MS Word)
- *Harvesting Web Resources* booklet (MS Word)
- *Web Browsing with Internet Explorer & Managing Favorites* booklet (MS Word)
- Project 7 Evaluation (MS Word)

Project 8

- Project 8 Completion Certificate (MS Word)
- Project 8 Completion 'Star' Certificate (MS Word)
- Project 8 Evaluation (MS Word)

Project 9

- Project 9 Completion Certificate (MS Word)
- Project 9 Completion 'Star' Certificate (MS Word)
- Project 9 Evaluation (MS Word)

Project 10

- Project 10 Completion Certificate (MS Word)
- Project 10 Completion 'Star' Certificate (MS Word)
- *Harvesting Web Resources* booklet (MS Word)
- *Web Browsing with Internet Explorer & Managing Favorites* booklet (MS Word)
- Project 10 Evaluation (MS Word)

Acknowledgements

The author and publishers gratefully acknowledge permission to use images from the following parties:

Data Harvest Group Ltd, 1 Eden Court, Leighton Buzzard, Bedfordshire LU7 4FY Tel: 01525 373666. www.data-harvest.co.uk (See Project 9 – Sensing Science Primary Graph Software).

Research Machines plc, New Mill House, 183 Milton Park, Abingdon, Oxfordshire OX14 4SE. Tel: 01235 823352. www.rm.com (See Projects 1 & 3 – Easitech screenshots, Figs 1.8, 1.9, 3.20.)

Introduction

This book is based on the belief that the integration of information and communication technology (ICT) and subject teaching is of benefit to children's development through the Foundation Stage, Key Stage 1 and Key Stage 2. It focuses on ICT in the context of science. By incorporating some of the powerful ICT tools described in this book in your science planning, the quality of your teaching and children's learning will improve. Similarly, by contextualising the children's ICT experience in meaningful science projects, children's ICT capability will be enhanced and extended. *Learning ICT with Science* is one of a series of ICT books: Teaching ICT through the Primary Curriculum. The core book in the series, *Progression in Primary ICT*, provides a more detailed discussion of the philosophy behind the approach and offers an overview and a planning matrix for all the projects described in the series.

The activities that are presented here offer practical guidance and suggestions for both teachers and trainees. For experienced teachers and practitioners there are ideas for ways that ICT can be developed through the areas of learning and the primary science curriculum using ICT tools with which you are familiar. For less confident or less experienced users of ICT there are recommendations for resources and step-by-step guides aimed at developing your confidence and competence with ICT as you prepare the activities for your children.

The relationship to the Foundation Stage areas of learning and National Curriculum Programmes of Study (PoS) for Science and ICT is described for each project. In some activities, such as Project 4: *Branching databases* and Project 10: *Using search engines*, the emphasis is on finding things out with ICT. The *Digital microscope* project offers opportunities for developing ideas and in the *Data logging* project the focus is on making things happen using ICT tools. Children are provided with purposeful opportunities to exchange and share information in Project 7: *Multimedia information source* and Project 3: *Concept cartoons*. Throughout all the projects, ways in which children can reflect on their use of ICT or explore its use in society are identified.

The projects do not provide an exhaustive or definitive list of ICT opportunities in primary science. Instead, they are tried and tested sequences of activities, adaptable across the age-range, which ensure that high quality learning in ICT is accompanied by high quality learning in science. The projects are closely linked to relevant units in the Qualifications and Curriculum Authority (QCA) schemes of work for science and ICT. They could be used to supplement, augment, extend or replace units in the ICT scheme of work. Although the projects are not future-proof, they have been designed to take advantage of some of the latest technologies now available in primary schools, such as interactive whiteboards, internet-linked computers and digital cameras.

A note on resources

Investment has improved the level of resources for the teaching of ICT in primary schools in recent years. The arrangement and availability of resources, however, still varies greatly from school to school. Some schools have invested heavily in centralised resources, setting up networked computer rooms or ICT suites. Others have gone down the route of networking the whole school, using wired or wireless technologies, with desktop or laptop computers being available in every classroom. Some schools have combined the two approaches, so that children have access to a networked suite and classroom computers. This book does not attempt to prescribe or promote a particular type of arrangement of computer hardware, but does make some assumptions in relation to the management of those resources. These assumptions are:

- The teacher has access to a large computer display for software demonstration and the sharing of children's work – this could be in the form of an interactive whiteboard (IWB), a data projector and large screen or a large computer monitor.
- Pupils (in groups or as individuals) have access to computers for hands-on activities – this may be in an ICT suite or by using a smaller number of classroom computers, perhaps on a rota basis.
- The school has internet access, and at least one networked computer is linked to a large display, as described above.
- Pupils have access to internet-linked computers and the school has a policy for safe use of the internet.
- Teachers and pupils have access to a range of software packages, including a web browser, 'office' software (such as a word processor) and some 'educational' software. Although this book makes some recommendations with regard to appropriate software, it also suggests alternatives that could be used if a specific package is not available.

The projects

Each project is presented using the following format:

- a Fact Card which gives a brief overview of the project content and how it links to curriculum requirements and documentation;
- guidance on how to teach a sequence of ICT activities in a subject context;
- information on pupils' prior learning required by the project;
- guidance for the teacher on the skills, knowledge and understandings required to teach the project, including step-by-step guidance on specific tasks, skills and tools;
- clear and specific information about what the children will learn in ICT and the subject;
- guidance on how to adapt the project for older or more experienced pupils;
- guidance on how to adapt the project for younger or less experienced pupils;
- a summary of reasons to teach the project, including reference to relevant curriculum documentation and research.

National Curriculum coverage

The ICT activities described in this book are those which are most relevant to science learning and hence not all areas of the ICT curriculum have been covered. The core text for the series, *Progression in Primary ICT*, shows how coverage of the ICT curriculum can be achieved by selecting the most appropriate subject-related activities for your teaching situation and how progression in ICT capability can be accomplished through meaningful contexts. Figure 1 provides an indication of the aspects of ICT which are addressed by the projects in this book.

Focus age groups for each project

Figure 2 provides an indication of the age group for which each project has been written. However, most activities can be adapted for older or younger children and guidance on how this can be done is provided in the information for each project.

Coverage of ICT National Curriculum Programmes of Study by each project

Key Stage 1

Projects:	1	2	3	4	5	6	7	8	9	10
Finding things out										
1a. gather information from a variety of sources		✓		✓						
1b. enter and store information in a variety of forms				✓						
1c. retrieve information that has been stored	✓			✓						
Developing ideas and making things happen										
2a. use text, tables, images and sound to develop their ideas			✓							
2b. select from and add to information they have retrieved for particular purposes										
2c. plan and give instructions to make things happen		✓								
2d. try things out and explore what happens in real and imaginary situations	✓	✓	✓	✓						
Exchanging and sharing information										
3a. share their ideas by presenting information in a variety of forms	✓		✓	✓						
3b. present their completed work effectively										

Key Stage 2

Projects:	1	2	3	4	5	6	7	8	9	10
Finding things out										
1a. talk about what information they need and how they can find and use it					✓	✓	✓	✓	✓	✓
1b. prepare information for development using ICT, including selecting suitable sources, finding information, classifying it and checking it for accuracy					✓	✓	✓	✓	✓	✓
1c. interpret information, to check it is relevant and reasonable and to think about what might happen if there were any errors or omissions					✓	✓	✓		✓	✓
Developing ideas and making things happen										
2a. develop and refine ideas by bringing together, organising and reorganising text, tables, images and sound as appropriate							✓	✓		✓
2b. create, test, improve and refine sequences of instructions to make things happen and to monitor events and respond to them									✓	
2c. use simulations and explore models in order to answer 'What if ... ?' questions, to investigate and evaluate the effect of changing values and to identify patterns and relationships										
Exchanging and sharing information										
3a. share and exchange information in a variety of forms, including e-mail					✓		✓	✓		✓
3b. be sensitive to the needs of the audience and think carefully about the content and quality when communicating information					✓		✓			✓

Figure 1

Year groups covered by each project

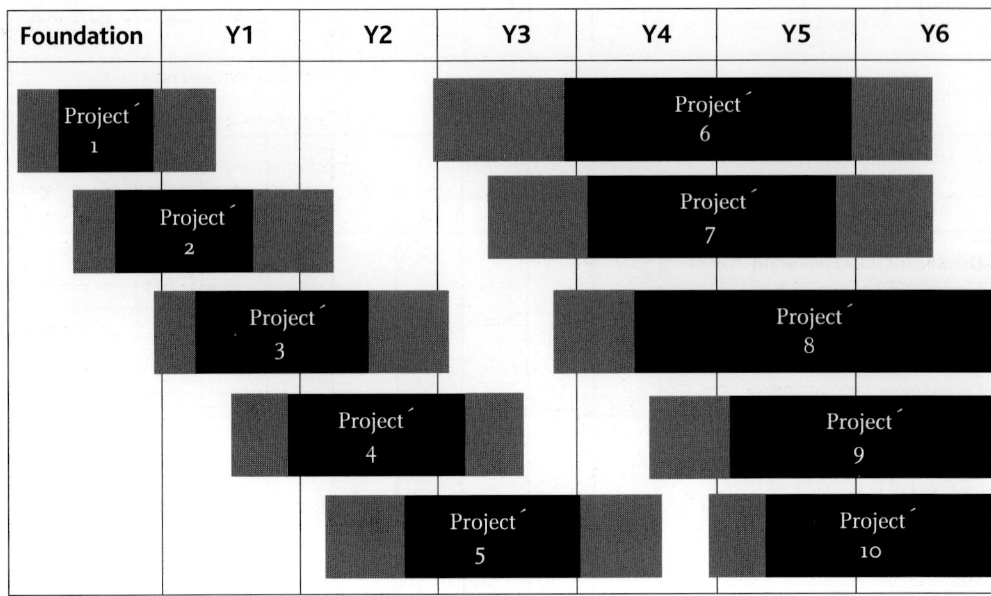

Figure 2

Links to the QCA scheme of work for ICT

Figure 3 indicates the relationship between the projects included in this book and the QCA ICT units in Key Stages 1 and 2. Three types of relationship are indicated in the table; projects which replace a unit, projects which support a unit and projects which extend a unit. By consulting Figure 3 it is possible to see at a glance which projects in this book could be used as an alternative to one of the QCA units. The projects which support units could be used alongside QCA units to reinforce, or revisit aspects of learning. For children who need additional challenges, it is possible to identify projects which extend the learning introduced in specific units of the QCA Scheme of Work.

Links to the QCA scheme of work for ICT in Key Stages 1 and 2

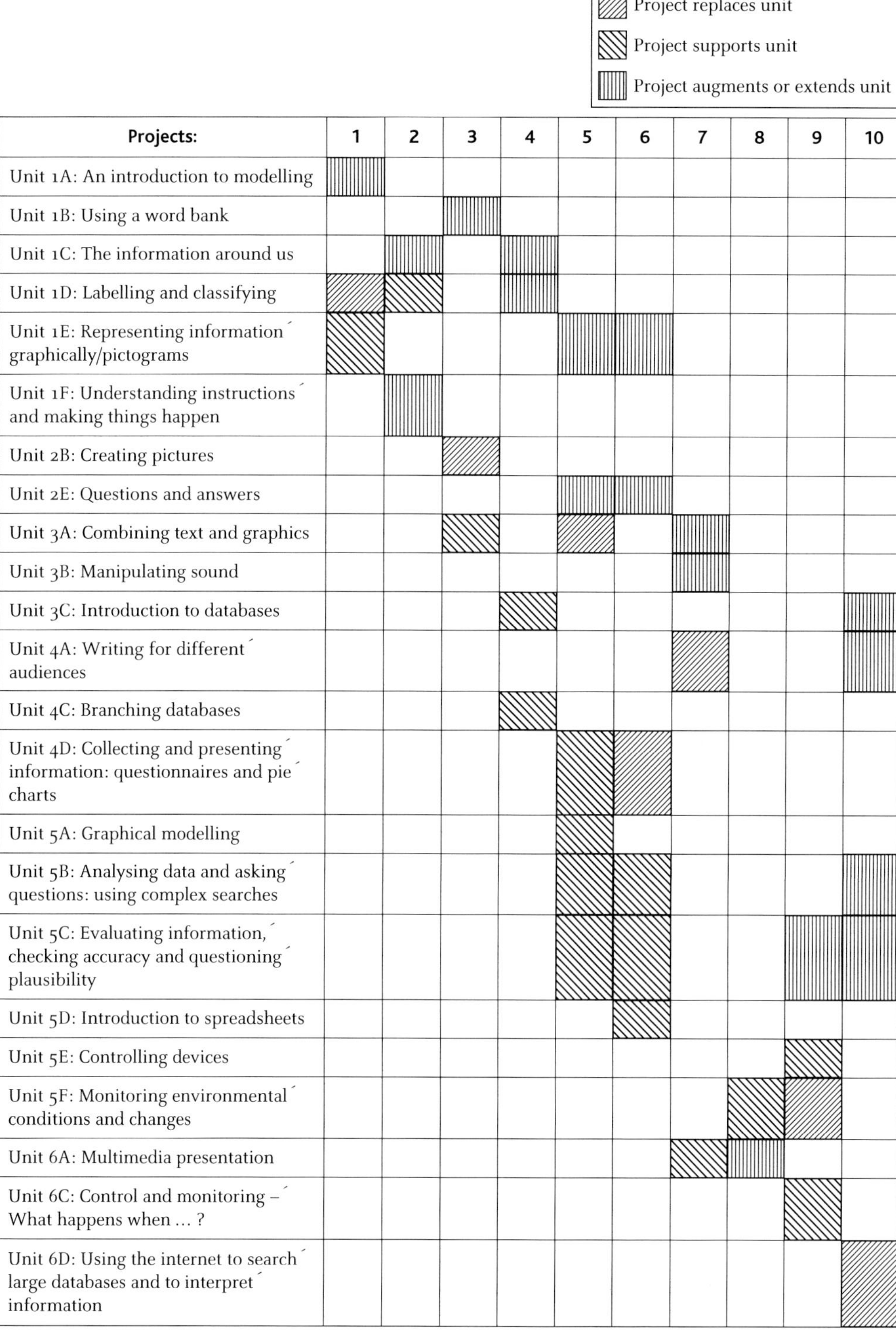

Key

- Project replaces unit
- Project supports unit
- Project augments or extends unit

Projects:	1	2	3	4	5	6	7	8	9	10
Unit 1A: An introduction to modelling	augments									
Unit 1B: Using a word bank			augments							
Unit 1C: The information around us		augments		augments						
Unit 1D: Labelling and classifying	replaces	supports		augments						
Unit 1E: Representing information graphically/pictograms	supports				augments	augments				
Unit 1F: Understanding instructions and making things happen		augments								
Unit 2B: Creating pictures			replaces							
Unit 2E: Questions and answers					augments	augments				
Unit 3A: Combining text and graphics			supports		replaces		augments			
Unit 3B: Manipulating sound							augments			
Unit 3C: Introduction to databases				supports						augments
Unit 4A: Writing for different audiences							replaces			augments
Unit 4C: Branching databases				supports						
Unit 4D: Collecting and presenting information: questionnaires and pie charts					supports	replaces				
Unit 5A: Graphical modelling					supports					
Unit 5B: Analysing data and asking questions: using complex searches					supports	supports				augments
Unit 5C: Evaluating information, checking accuracy and questioning plausibility					supports	supports			augments	augments
Unit 5D: Introduction to spreadsheets						supports				
Unit 5E: Controlling devices									supports	
Unit 5F: Monitoring environmental conditions and changes								supports	replaces	
Unit 6A: Multimedia presentation							supports	augments		
Unit 6C: Control and monitoring – What happens when … ?									supports	
Unit 6D: Using the internet to search large databases and to interpret information										replaces

Figure 3

Project Fact Card: Project 1: Drag and drop sorting

Who is it for?

- 4- to 5-year-olds (NC Level 1)

What will the children do?

- Select images on the screen and position them according to observable characteristics using pens or fingers on a whiteboard, a stylus on a tablet PC or the mouse or other input device on a PC

What should the children know already?

- That it is possible to interact with an image on the computer to make changes to it
- How to select an item on the screen

What do I need to know?

- How to search for and save images
- How to use basic draw tools to create simple shapes
- How to insert images
- How to lock objects to the page in drawing software

What resources will I need?

- Drawing software or whiteboard software which allows drag and drop
- Whiteboard, tablet PC or touch-screen will help

What will the children learn?

- That pictures provide information
- That objects can be described, identified and sorted using keywords
- That ICT can help to sort and present information
- That object-based drawing software can be used to model and present sorting activities
- That ICT can be used to communicate ideas through pictures
- That ICT makes it easy to correct mistakes and explore alternatives

How to challenge the more able

- Help children to devise and create their own sorting sheets
- Encourage and support children to find their own images to add to the exercise
- The sorting can be extended to two functions and Venn diagrams or Carroll diagrams introduced
- Work with a very similar group of objects to encourage careful observation of differences

How to support the less able

- Provide a simplified collection of images
- Make sure that the images and diagrams are large and clear
- Physically support the movement of images

Why teach this?

- The activity in this project is designed to emulate an activity that the children should be familiar with using concrete apparatus.
- The main focus of the activity is the FS Area of Learning 'Knowledge and understanding of the world' as the children explore and examine objects, sorting them by one function, and find out about ICT.
- They will operate simple equipment and develop an interest in the technology.
- It is possible to carry out this activity using images of almost any collection of objects. They could be photographs of animals or insects, even the children themselves. The internet is also a useful source of images; the process of sorting and presenting the information can be carried out using things that the children are interested in, e.g. vehicles, cartoon characters, food, fruit.

PROJECT 1

Drag and drop sorting

What will the children do?

The provisional nature of ICT that enables interaction with images to change their layout and appearance is key to the sorting activity in this project. As well as developing the children's knowledge and understanding of the objects that they are sorting, they will be developing skills controlling the software and understanding of the functions of the technology. There are opportunities to contribute to physical development through the necessary motor control of the mouse, touchpad, stylus and interactive whiteboard.

There are several commercial sorting games available and by using software such as *Flash* or *Hot Potatoes – JMatch* it is possible to create drag and drop exercises which offer feedback to the children by not allowing 'incorrect' placing of images and praising 'correct' ones. While there may be advantages to these types of ICT resource when a practitioner is unable to observe, in a practitioner-led group activity, the facility to place objects anywhere on the screen and discuss the children's reasons makes a valuable contribution to learning and assessment.

The type of draw file described in this project is easily created and has the advantage of being tailored to the needs, interests and environment of the children.

Activity 1: Drag and drop sorting

The key Foundation Stage activity is the sorting of objects by one function. Clearly the sorting of screen-based images needs to complement hands-on activities with physical objects but can extend the activity to objects that would be hard to obtain or difficult or dangerous to handle.

Whether the images are on the whiteboard or computer screen the activity requires the children to select images and move them to the appropriate part of the screen using the pen or finger on the interactive whiteboard or the mouse or other input device on the computer.

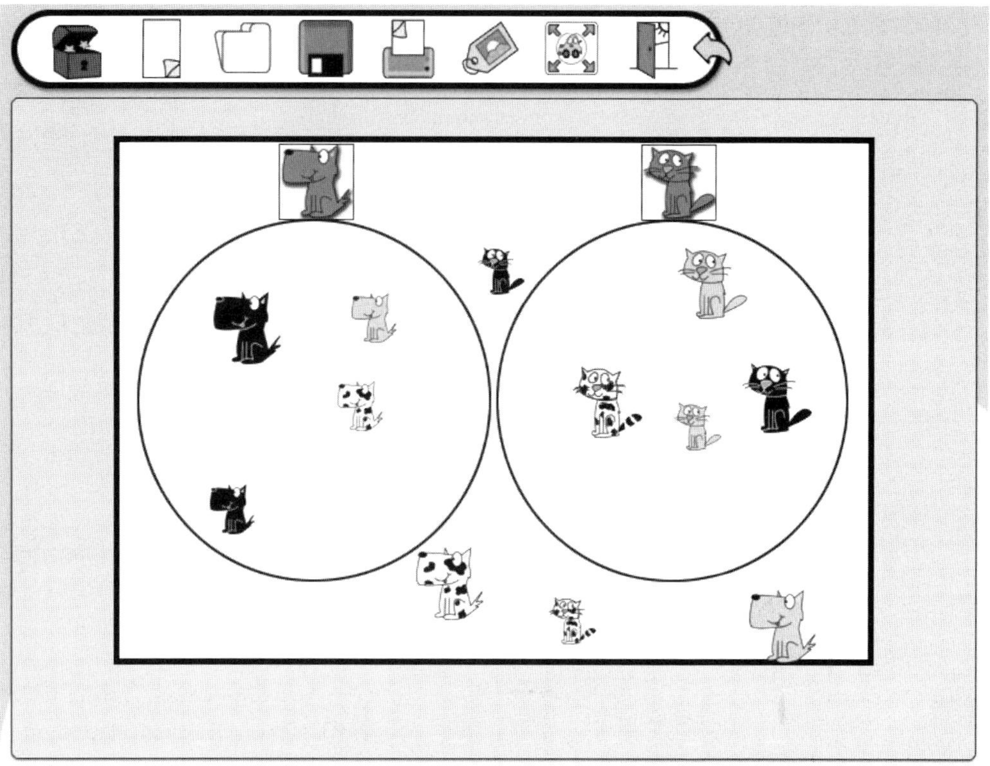

A sorting exercise using BlackCat Sort *on the interactive whiteboard*

What should the children know already?

While some understanding that it is possible to interact with an image on the computer to make changes to it will help the children to focus on the objects, it is not essential. Similarly, some understanding of 'point and click' to select an item on the screen will help, but this activity could equally serve as an introduction to computer use. Whatever the children's prior knowledge, their development will be aided by including some discussion of the role of the technology in the activity and how the children managed to control it.

What do I need to know?

The resource for this activity can be created using any drawing software or general purpose software like *Microsoft Word* or *Textease*. All interactive whiteboards come with software tools and there is a growing range of interactive whiteboard teaching tools like *Lesson Planit* and *Easiteach* which enable the creation of this type of resource. The examples here use *Easiteach* and *Textease* but any software which will enable images to be imported, selected and moved will work.

How to search for and save images

Most drawing software will come with a range of images. Whiteboard software, too, prides itself on the range of visual resources supplied with the software for teachers and practitioners to use. If, however, you cannot locate the image that you require, there are several avenues open to you.

- Search online using a search engine like Google images
- Photograph the object using a digital camera
- Scan pictures from books or magazines

Whatever the source, the resultant image files need to be saved to disk so that they can be inserted in the document. *Textease* and *Easiteach* use the same resource banks so a collection of images can be saved in the **Clip Art** directory and used in either program. The easiest way to transfer images is by opening two windows: one for the source – in this case the digital camera:

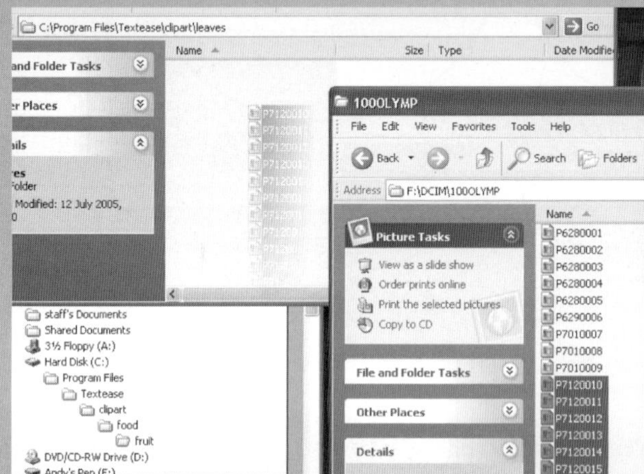

> Copy or Move?
>
> When dragging files from one window to another, one of two things will happen.
>
> 1. If both windows are from the same disk the file will be moved.
> 2. If the windows are from different disks the file will be copied.

and the other for the destination folder or directory on the local disk or network server. The images that you require can then be selected and dragged to the destination folder window. Creating a separate folder for each collection of images makes it easier to locate and insert them later on. Files can be transferred one at a time or the entire contents of a window can be selected by clicking on **Select All** in the **Edit** menu. It is also possible to select a group by 'lassoing' them – click on the white space beside the first file that you require and drag down to select the rest of the group.

How to use basic draw tools to create simple shapes

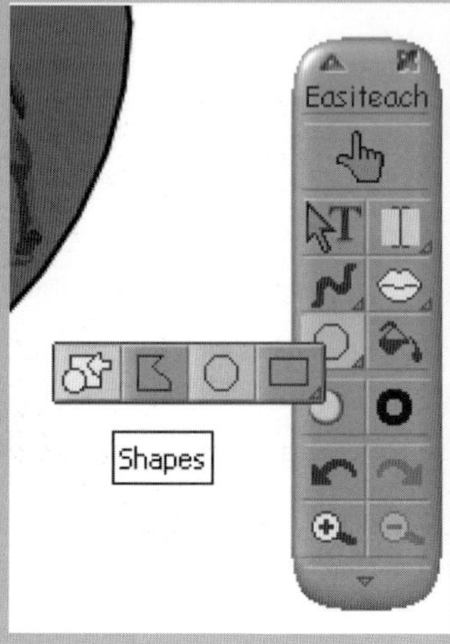

With the images saved a screen can be prepared as elaborate or simple as required. If the children have been sorting objects using hoops, then a simple circle would be all that is needed to get started. All whiteboard and drawing software should allow you to select a circle or rectangle drawing tool and create the shape by clicking and dragging.

Once drawn, the shape can be resized, relocated or edited. To select the shape you may need to click

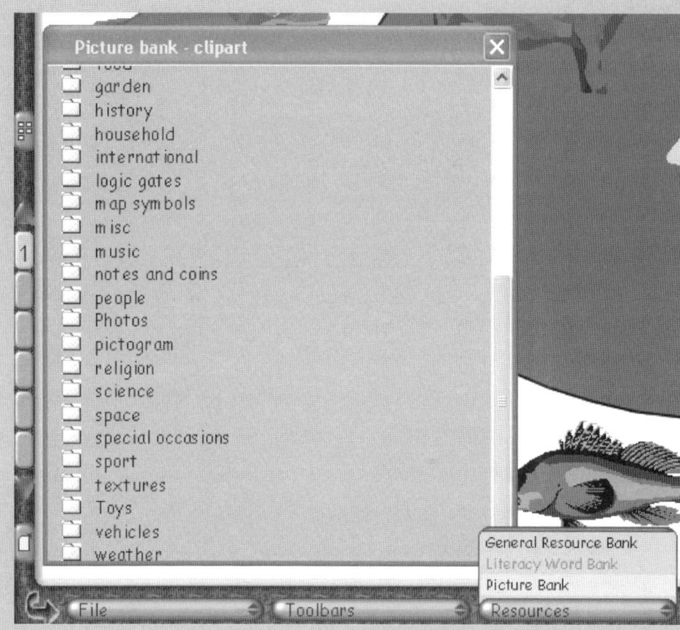

precisely on a line, not in the middle of it. Once selected, square or circular 'handles' should appear at each corner which can be clicked and dragged to resize the shape. *Textease* and *Easiteach* also have a green 'handle' that can be dragged to rotate the shape.

Once the diagram is created, text can be added, if required, by selecting the **T** text tool and clicking on the page before typing. Double clicking on text will select the text for editing in the same way as the shapes were. With the diagram complete, the images to be sorted can be added.

How to insert images

If the images have been saved into the software resources folder, then selecting **Picture Bank** from the **Resources** menu in *Easiteach*, or clicking on the 'choose a picture' icon in *Textease*, will open a new window displaying the categories of pictures available. If your pictures are located elsewhere on the computer, the drop down menu available next to the title of the Clip Art folder allows you to navigate through the files on your computer.

Once the folder of images that you saved earlier is visible, the images can be added to the file simply by clicking and dragging them from the **Picture Bank** window onto your diagram.

Pictures can either be positioned on the page in a start position ready for the children to move and then the **Picture Bank** window can be closed, or the children could be encouraged to choose an image from the **Picture bank** and drag it from there to the appropriate area of the diagram.

How to lock objects to the page in drawing software

Because both the images and the diagram are 'draggable' objects, there is a danger that the children may select parts of the diagram and move them by mistake. The way to avoid this happening is to lock the diagram, and any text that you wish to be fixed, to the page background. In *Textease* this is achieved by selecting the item so that the 'handles' are visible and then selecting **Lock to page** from the **Tools** menu.

In *Easiteach* the spanner-shaped **Utilities** icon must be selected from the main toolbar to show the additional utilities. With the shape that you wish to lock selected, click on the padlock icon. As soon as you click somewhere else on the page to de-select the shape it is locked to the page and cannot be selected. If you subsequently find that you need to edit the shape, you can unlock all locked items by selecting **Access locked items** from the **Tools** menu in *Textease* or by clicking on the key icon adjacent to the padlock on the **Utilities** toolbar in *Easiteach*.

NOTE:
Remember to click on **Access locked items** again once editing is complete to remove the permission.

If you do want to create 'self-marking' drag and drop exercises, you can use *Hot Potatoes' – JMatch* from Half-Baked Software available at http://web.uvic.ca/hrd/hotpot/

Example Textease files are provided on the CD-ROM accompanying this book to enable you to experiment.

What will the children learn?

That pictures provide information

By helping to create a record of their sorting, the children are both seeing pictures as information and using them to communicate new information.

That objects can be described, identified and sorted using keywords

Whether the words are written or not, the sorting will revolve around a criterion or function of the images selected. The consistent use of language by the practitioner is vital if the idea of keywords is going to take root. To challenge children's ability to observe closely, banks of images can be selected that are very similar. Children can also be challenged to decide on the sorting criteria or use the resource to play a guessing game. Sort the pictures and see if the children can work out which criteria or keyword you have used.

That ICT can help to sort and present information

The similarities and differences between carrying out this kind of activity with picture cards on the floor and with drawing software on a screen need to be discussed. Previous sorting exercises can be saved, revisited and altered and printed out to explore the role of ICT.

That object-based drawing software can be used to model and present sorting activities

The process of modelling with ICT, where children are able to try things out, make decisions and communicate their ideas, is a powerful tool to put in the hands of young learners. By integrating the sorting of physical objects with this activity, the idea of the computer being able to represent tasks that can be carried out in other ways will begin to develop.

That ICT can be used to communicate ideas through pictures

Sharing printouts of their sorting activity will enable the children to talk to others about the activity and the outcome. By taking digital photographs of familiar locations or objects and involving children in the classification and layout of the sorting diagram, they can begin to see how the positioning of pictures can convey information.

That ICT makes it easy to correct mistakes and explore alternatives

Although this is an often cited benefit of ICT the emphasis is usually on the creation of a 'perfect' piece of work. No matter how many errors are made along the way, they are invisible once corrected. The real value for learning is the potential that the technology offers to encourage children to explore and try out their ideas, secure in the knowledge that they can reverse decisions.

Challenging the more able and supporting the less able: modifying the project for older and younger pupils

Through providing a simplified collection of images that relate to the child's interest or experience it is possible to help to motivate children who would struggle with this task. Also by selecting images from the picture bank with the children, the task can be fine tuned to individuals. If children struggle with interpretation or selection, enlarge images and diagrams to ensure that they are clear enough for the size of screen that you are using. Increasing the line thickness will help children whose fine motor control makes it difficult for them to select the shape that they need. For those children still developing the necessary control to position the images, physically supporting their movement with shared control of the mouse or pen would be a way to start. Some argue that the larger scale of the interactive whiteboard can help to develop the physical control required and makes this type of activity possible for children who would have difficulties coping with a mouse and small screen, for example. While this can be the case, the exercise of dragging can prove difficult when little fingers lose contact with the whiteboard. Putting finger puppets on can increase the size of children's fingers and reduce the friction for dragging operations. It is also possible to carry out this type of activity using *MyWorlds*, which overcomes the dragging problems by enabling an object to be 'picked up' by a click of the mouse and 'carried' until the mouse is clicked again. It is necessary to guard against learning opportunities being denied to the children by too much assistance, however.

Children who have risen to the challenge can be helped to devise and create their own sorting sheets, initially by altering the sorting criterion or by changing the design of the sorting diagram. They may be encouraged to go on to add a further shape for another criterion. Some children may be able to find their own images to add to the exercise – either from books or magazines that could be scanned or by taking the digital camera and choosing objects to photograph. If you find that children are focusing on surface features such as colour and you want them to look more closely, work with a very similar group of objects to encourage careful observation of differences. Discussion of a related set of animals or plants, for example, will also challenge and develop language as differences become more difficult to describe.

A minority of children may enjoy the challenge of a more complex sorting activity extended to include two functions or characteristics. The type of sorting or classification like the example with leaves below has traditionally used Venn diagrams or Carroll diagrams to record the task, but children's representations are equally valid.

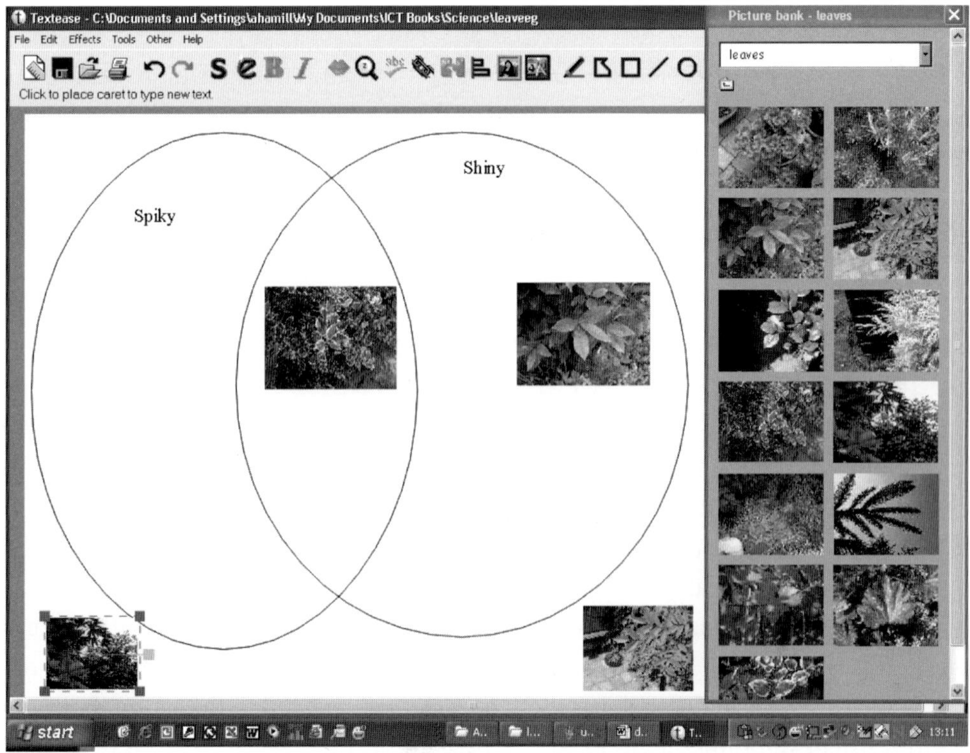

Adding pictures to a Venn diagram using Textease

Why teach this?

The activity in this project is designed to model sorting games using concrete materials, which should be familiar to the children. The main focus of the task is the development of their knowledge and understanding of the world as the children explore and examine objects, sorting them by one function and, in the process, finding out about ICT. They will operate simple ICT equipment and have the opportunity to develop an interest in the technology as they do so. It is possible to create models for the children to carry out the process of sorting and presenting information using images of almost any collection of objects. Ideally collections that the children are interested in, e.g. animals, insects, vehicles, food, fruit, clothes, even the children themselves, will work best. The images could be photographs, Clip Art or scanned images; the internet is also a useful source. By involving children in the gathering of images from a variety of sources, opportunities for them to find out about the potential of ICT to manipulate and process images will also be presented.

This kind of activity aims to build on the scientific curiosity that young learners have and can be used to challenge children's views –

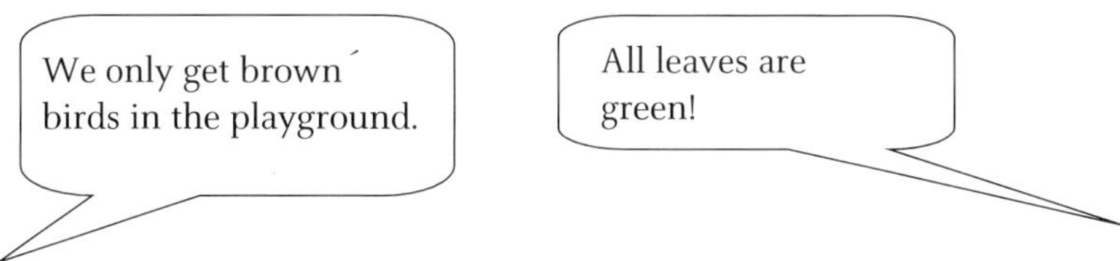

We only get brown birds in the playground.
All leaves are green!

The activity can, and should, promote a spirit of enquiry and develop investigative skills and a knowledge of ICT tools that will help young learners begin to understand the scientific process which is at the heart of National Curriculum science.

See also *Humanities* Project 1 (*Decision making with a mouse*) and *Arts* Project 1 (*Building pictures*) for related activities.

Project Fact Card: Project 2: Digital microscope – time-lapse

Who is it for?

- 4- to 5-year-olds (NC Level 1)

What will the children do?

- As part of a group the children will use a digital microscope and interactive whiteboard to observe and capture images of small creatures. Some will go on to set up the digital microscope to record images automatically

What should the children know already?

- That objects can be made to look bigger without changing their actual size
- That clicking on parts of the screen can make things happen

What do I need to know?

- How to connect the digital microscope to the computer
- How to focus the microscope and adjust magnification
- How to change the lighting of a specimen
- How to capture still images
- How to capture video
- How to set up the software to create a time-lapse film

What resources will I need?

- Digital microscope and software
- Interactive whiteboard

What will the children learn?

- That information can be collected from pictures and can be presented in a variety of forms
- To use ICT to test a hypothesis
- That computers can represent real situations
- That devices that carry out repeated actions follow stored instructions which can include numbers
- That control devices must be programmed

How to challenge the more able

- Let them choose their own creatures to watch
- Encourage them to capture and save images independently
- Encourage them to set up their own time-lapse experiments

How to support the less able

- Talk to them about the role of the technology in capturing and magnifying the images of the creatures
- Guide them as they capture images of the creatures

Why teach this?

- The project is targeted on the FS Area of Learning 'Knowledge and understanding of the world' both in terms of its ICT and science content. The children will learn how to operate equipment as they perform simple functions on ICT apparatus and find out about the uses of technology to support their learning. The project also addresses the KS1 ICT NC as the children explore information from different sources and learn that information exists in different forms. Some will also recognise that the microscope through the computer responds to signals and instructions.
- The project can contribute to, or prepare for, the teaching of QCA ICT Scheme of Work Units 1C, 1D and 1F.
- The children are encouraged to make observations as the ability to see the creatures in close-up can produce evidence to answer questions and stimulate their interest and curiosity. The activity helps to teach investigative skills listed in the Science NC KS1 PoS – particularly using first-hand experience (Sc1, 2b), recording observations (Sc1, 2f) and making simple comparisons (Sc1, 2h). Gathering information in this way helps them to see images as information. There are plenty of opportunities for children to raise questions and test them through investigation and observation as they examine living things to find out more about them. It can also make a valuable contribution to Sc2: *Life processes and living things* and the QCA Science Scheme of Work Unit 2B.

PROJECT 2

Digital microscope – time-lapse

What will the children do?

The digital microscope is a fantastic piece of equipment, especially for young learners. It makes it possible for children in the early years to experience and wonder at the intricate details of tiny creatures at first hand, without having to learn how to shut one eye or control their blinking! As part of Science Year (2001–2) every school in the UK was provided with an *Intel QX3* computer microscope with very easily operated software. As well as providing magnification, the microscope brings the same benefits to teaching and learning as digital video – that is, things which happen too quickly for children to see can be slowed down or 'freeze-framed' and those things which happen too slowly can, through time-lapse photography, be speeded up.

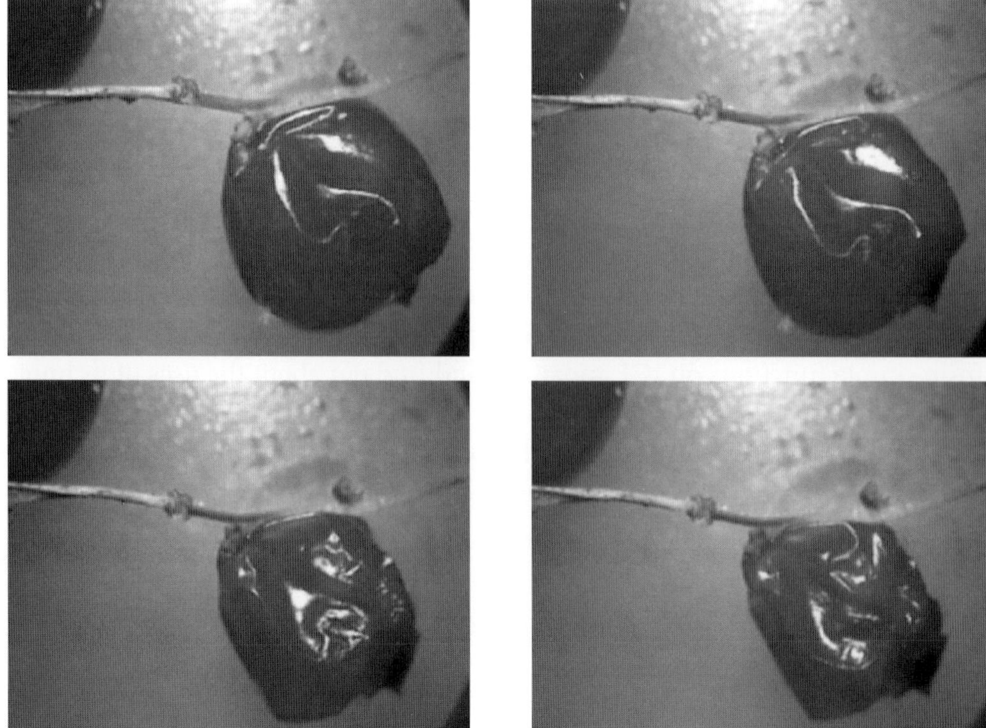

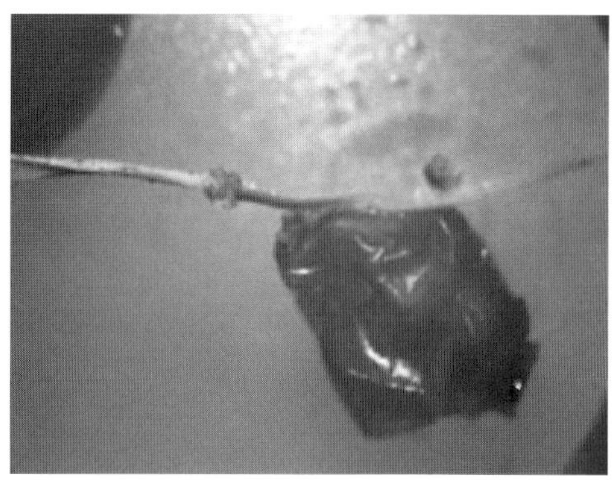

A sequence of frames from a time-lapse movie

Activity 1: First capture your 'minibeast'

Using a shallow container with a lid, small live creatures are captured humanely and placed under the microscope for short periods of time. Either using the video or still image snapshot tool, pictures of the 'minibeasts' are saved to the computer.

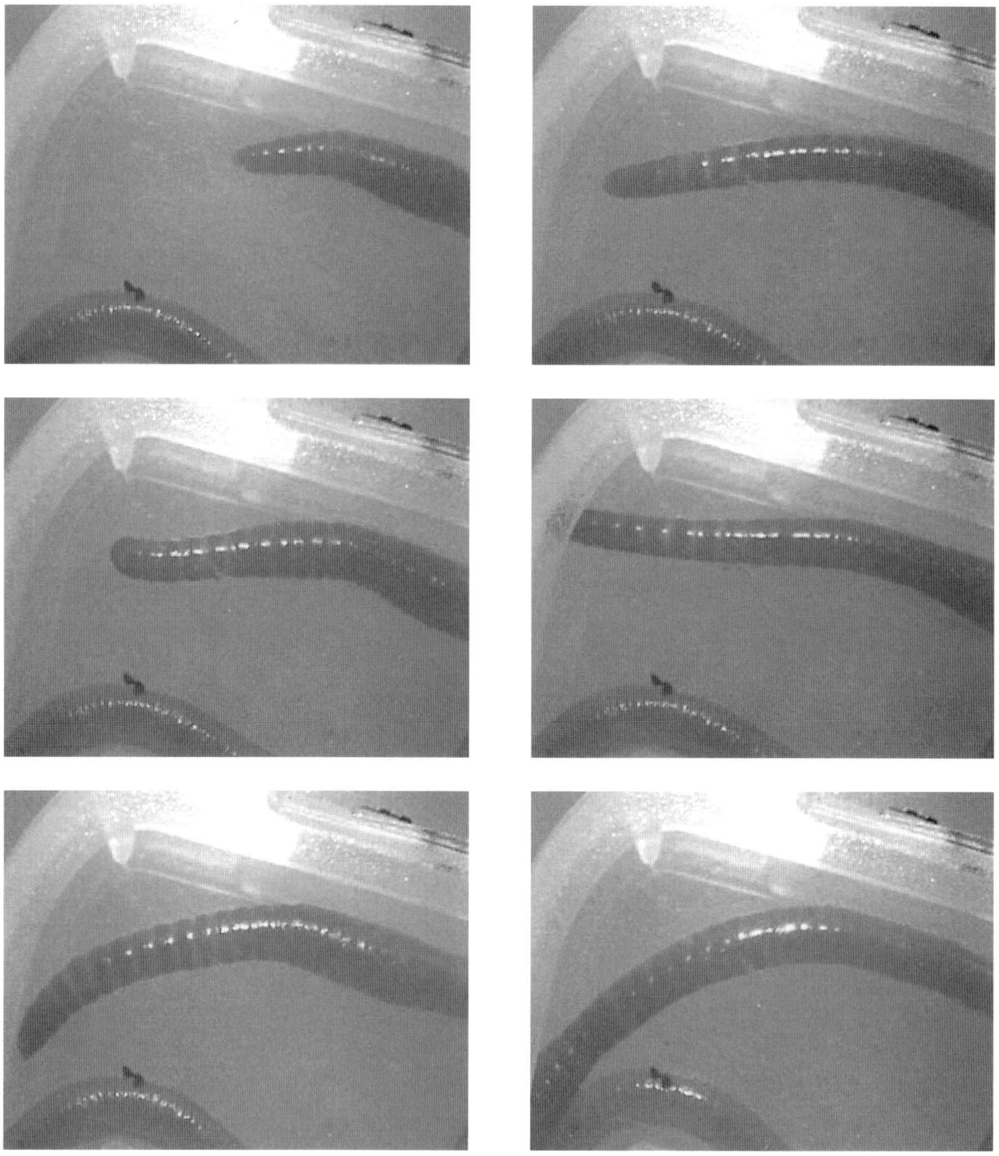

Activity 2: Spot the difference

Using the still image and video files saved to the computer, observations and discussions about the main parts of the animals, their similarities and differences can be undertaken. The need to treat animals with care and how the technology helps us to observe details without causing suffering to the animals are valuable facets to this activity.

What should the children know already?

As an adult-led activity it is possible to undertake this task with children who have little or no ICT capability. By the adult modelling ICT use and explaining and showing the functions of the microscope, the children will begin to develop their knowledge of ways that ICT can help them learn.

Recording a time-lapse movie using Intel QX3 software

The software has been developed for a young audience and children will soon know which buttons to press to take photographs.

That objects can be made to look bigger without changing their actual size

Although nearly all children are familiar with close-up and zoom effects from watching television, some preparation for seeing a two-metre-long earwig on the interactive whiteboard is advisable! Taking a pencil or small inanimate object and placing it under the microscope first will help the children to predict how big their 'minibeast' is going to appear when the digital microscope images are viewed on the screen.

That clicking on parts of the screen can make things happen

Using an interactive whiteboard is more intuitive for young learners than using a mouse as they are able to physically touch the 'buttons' on the screen to control the microscope and make recordings. If the activity is to be carried out with young learners using a PC, it would be worth considering a tablet PC, which can be operated via the screen. Familiarity with ICT conventions of this sort is soon gained, however, if children have little previous experience.

What do I need to know?

How to connect the digital microscope to the computer

With the advent of Universal Serial Bus (USB) ports, connecting peripheral devices such as the digital microscope to a computer has become relatively easy. Make sure the software has been installed on the computer before you connect the microscope for the first time because a piece of software called a driver is needed to make sure that any device is able to communicate effectively with the computer and vice versa. Once the software has been installed the USB lead from the camera (a) is connected to the USB port on the computer (b) as shown in image c.

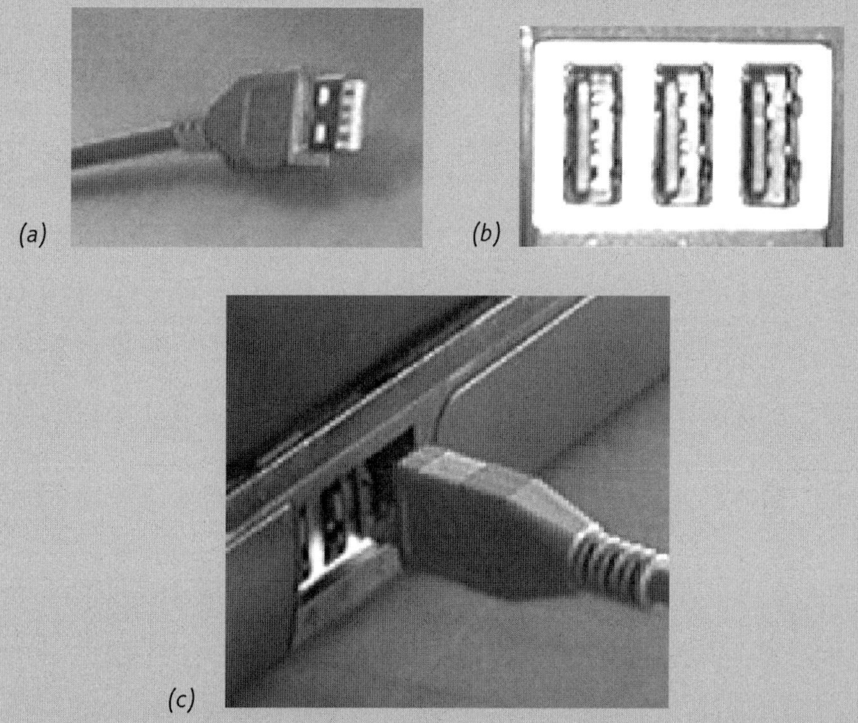

(a) (b) (c)

Notice that while the plugs are rectangular, they can only be inserted one way round. Once connected, the computer may make a warning sound and indicate, via a small callout window, that the microscope has been detected and that it is installed ready for use.

How to focus the microscope and adjust magnification

The Intel Play QX3 Computer Microscope software, when launched, will display whatever has been placed on the platform. The focus and magnification can be controlled by using the microscope controls. The green horizontal wheel is rotated to change the magnification from × 10 to × 60 to × 200. The current magnification is clearly marked on the wheel itself. To obtain the sharpest image the blue control knobs either side of the microscope are turned to raise or lower the platform and bring the sample into focus.

How to change the lighting of a specimen

The microscope has a top and bottom light. The top light comes on automatically if you remove the microscope from its stand. The bottom light is for viewing translucent objects. The direction and intensity of the lighting is adjusted easily using the software. If you run the software with a sample on the platform and microscope connected, it will automatically open in Live View displaying what is currently visible. The light adjustment tools are displayed to the right of the image window. The direction of the light is chosen by clicking on the top or bottom lightbulb icons – the light which you choose should be clearly visible on the microscope. Watch the image on the screen as you make adjustments; clicking and dragging the green slider icon will fade or brighten the selected light source. Watch for a few moments after making changes, as the software will take a short while to respond.

How to capture still images

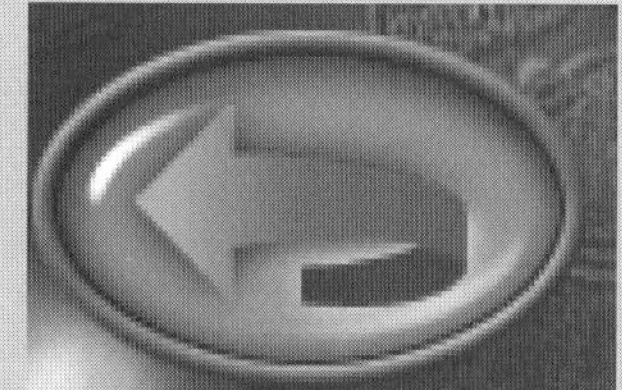

While observing either objects or moving creatures on the screen in Live Mode it is possible to capture still images by clicking on the Snapshot tool. Images are automatically saved to the Collection page which is accessible from the main screen.

To access the main screen click on the arrow in the bottom left corner of the Live Mode screen. The Collection button reveals all the images and video clips that have been recorded.

How to capture video

Short clips of video can be recorded by clicking on the 'record movie' icon when you observe something interesting happening in Live Mode. The action will be recorded until you click the button (which will now display 'stop record') again. The video clips can be viewed frame by frame or exported from the software from the main page.

How to set up the software to create a time-lapse film

For slow-moving subjects or processes the software can be set up to take one frame at a time at intervals of between 1 second and 1 hour. So long as there is enough available memory to store the images, events lasting several days can be captured in this way. The resulting movie can then be viewed at normal speed, so that the action appears to be accelerated, or one frame at a time to discuss the stages separately.

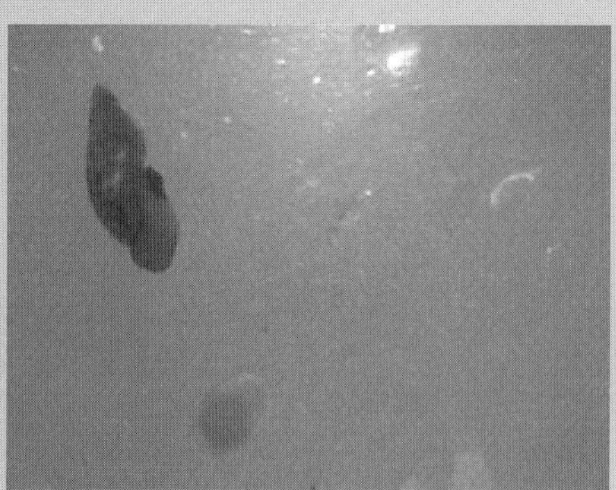

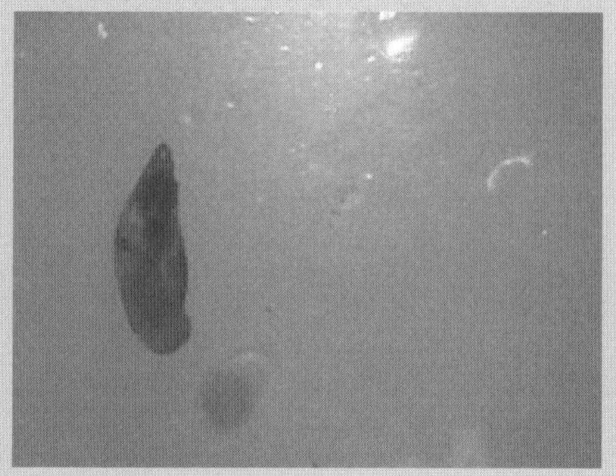

To set up a time-lapse video film click on the Time Lapse icon on the Live View screen to reveal the controls.

Choose the interval between shots by dragging the slider to the right to increase it and to the left to decrease it. The interval is displayed in the setting window. With your chosen slothful creature in view, click the Record button to start. The time elapsed is displayed beneath the 'stop record' icon and the number of snapshots taken is recorded. The computer will continue to record one frame at a time at the interval that you have set until the 'stop record' button is pressed.

The video can then be viewed straight away and is automatically stored on the Collection page. Any images or videos can be exported from the software as JPEG or AVI files so that they can be accessed on any Windows computer.

Example AVI files are provided on the CD-ROM accompanying this book.

What will the children learn?

That information can be collected from pictures and can be presented in a variety of forms

The recognition that these pictures represent facts and provide information is important for the children. Printing out and comparing still images of worms moving, for example, will enable simple comparisons or measurements to be made of changes in width as the worm moves.

To use ICT to test a hypothesis

Encouraging children to make predictions about what they think will happen is important for science development as well as providing revealing assessment information. Estimates of measurement of size or distance or even time can be made and tested through time-lapse films.

That computers can represent real situations

The ability for the children to observe changes on the microscope platform and on the screen will help them to recognise the reality of the images. The control of the lights, for example, can also be observed on the screen and the microscope.

That devices that carry out repeated actions follow stored instructions which can include numbers

Setting up the microscope for a time-lapse film is a type of simple program. Introducing the children to 'control stories' or instructions, while not necessary for this activity, is good groundwork for later control work. Tell the children to imagine that the microscope is a robot and to give it instructions orally, encouraging them to be as precise as possible.

That control devices must be programmed

Without precise instructions and also telling the microscope when to start by clicking on the Record button, the pictures would not be recorded. The software also usefully makes sounds each time a picture is taken so the children can observe that their instructions are being carried out.

Challenging the more able and supporting the less able: modifying the project for older and younger pupils

It is possible, with this type of project, for children to be quite passive in their use of the technology. Working alongside the less experienced children, guiding them as they capture images of the creatures and ensuring that they all have opportunity to control both the microscope and the software, is important if the project is to make a difference to children's ICT capability. Through talking to children about the role of the technology in capturing and magnifying the images of the creatures, there are ways that elements of National Curriculum (NC) ICT Level 1 can be developed and assessed as the children talk about ICT use and make choices – between video or still image, for example – and come to recognise the way that the microscope responds to signals and instructions.

For more able children, increased choices can be made by letting them choose their own creatures and respond to interests that they have. Listen for questions or theories that the children raise which could be investigated using the microscope. If children can control and navigate around the software, then they can be encouraged to capture and save images independently and even to set up their own time-lapse experiments. There are opportunities to contribute to NC ICT Level 2 if children can plan their own investigation and describe the effects of their actions.

Why teach this?

The project is targeted on the Foundation Stage Area of Learning 'Knowledge and understanding of the world' both in terms of its ICT and science content. The children will learn how to operate equipment as they perform simple functions, both operating the microscope and using the software, and, in so doing, will find out about the uses of technology to support their learning. The project also addresses the Key Stage 1 ICT NC as the children explore information from different sources and learn that information exists in different forms including still and moving images. Some children will also recognise that the microscope through the computer responds to signals and instructions as they become involved in setting up and recording a time-lapse film.

Several QCA ICT Scheme of Work units can be supported or replaced by using the digital microscope. The tasks relate to QCA ICT Units 1C: *The information around us* and 1F: *Understanding instructions and making things happen.* Unit 1D: *Labelling and classifying* is also a relevant activity for some of the types of scientific investigation involving the digital microscope.

The children are encouraged to make careful observations in any of the digital microscope activities as the ability to see the creatures in close-up can produce evidence to answer their questions and stimulate their interest and curiosity. The activity helps to teach investigative skills listed in the Science NC KS1 PoS – particularly using first-hand experience (Sc1, 2b), recording observations (Sc1, 2f) and making simple comparisons (Sc1, 2h). Gathering information in this way helps the children to see images as information and extends the range of equipment that they can suggest to help them investigate. There are plenty of opportunities for children to raise questions and test them through investigation and observation as they examine living things to find out more about them. The microscope can not only make tiny things visible but it also helps to share the observations with the whole class, either through a data projector or by placing captured images and video on the network or individual computers. Depending on the area of science knowledge under investigation, it can make a valuable contribution to Sc2: *Life processes and living things,* by looking at small creatures, or Sc3: *Materials and their properties,* by looking at the structure of fabrics or evaporating liquids using time-lapse photography. The QCA Science Scheme of Work Unit 2B: *Plants and animals in the local environment* would be enhanced by incorporating this type of activity.

Project Fact Card: Project 3: Concept cartoons

Who is it for?

- 6- to 7-year-olds (NC Levels 1–2)

What will the children do?

- This project enables the children to use a range of word-processing and formatting tools to present and communicate their understanding through creating a cartoon of an everyday event with a scientific explanation. The activities in the project can be easily differentiated by handing over different amounts of each task for the children to complete

What do I need to know?

- How to insert pictures into a word-processed document
- How to use simple draw tools to create speech bubbles
- How to group drawing objects
- How to order drawing objects one behind the other
- How to create text boxes
- How to set up a word bank
- How to use the interactive whiteboard to add text

What should the children know already?

- How to input text
- How to select objects – in this case words from a word bank – by moving the mouse and clicking

What resources will I need?

- Word processor with some drawing tools and word bank facility
- Clip Art
- Interactive whiteboard

What will the children learn?

- That ICT can be used to create pictures to present information
- To use ICT appropriately to communicate ideas through text and images
- That ICT makes it easy to correct mistakes and explore alternatives
- That computers use icons to provide information and instructions

How to challenge the more able

- Involve more able children in all aspects of the creation of the cartoon – even helping to create a word bank
- Suggest they make their own drawings either using *Paint* software or scanning in original artwork

How to support the less able

- Provide software that supports word banks and create a bank of vocabulary for the children to use
- Type ideas for them
- Use children's drawings as a part of the cartoon

Why teach this?

- As well as contributing to NC ICT these activities lend themselves to collaborative discussion, around a computer monitor or interactive whiteboard, that will promote and explore children's understanding of science. Depending upon the extent to which the children become involved in the creation of the cartoon, different elements of the ICT KS1 PoS will be addressed. All children will experience the use of ICT to exchange and share information (3a) and the creation of a cartoon will contribute to the development of ideas (2a, 2d).
- This project offers a context for elements of QCA ICT Scheme of Work Units 1B, 2B and 3A.
- As well as the area of science knowledge which is the focus of the cartoon, the project contributes to Science NC KS1 PoS statements Sc1, 2g, using ICT to communicate, and 2i, as they explain their expectations. It is possible to incorporate a concept cartoon activity of this sort into any of the QCA Science Scheme of Work units for KS1.

PROJECT 3

Concept cartoons

What will the children do?

Concept cartoons have become an effective approach to teaching, learning and assessment in science since they were created by Brenda Keogh and Stuart Naylor in 1991. They have since been developed commercially and several published resources exist. They are essentially cartoon drawings of people arguing about everyday events with scientific explanations. Through a small amount of dialogue the nub of a scientific idea is applied to everyday situations. The current scientific viewpoint is included as one of the suggestions and it is important that the alternative viewpoints presented are given equal status. This approach to learning has proved to be a useful tool for challenging ideas and promoting scientific discussion and also for assessment to elicit current understanding. Further information is available from the Association for Science Education (ASE) at www.ase.org.uk/ and www.conceptcartoons.com. Commercially produced interactive concept cartoons can be evaluated and purchased from www.conceptcartoons.com; however, buying cake does nothing to promote culinary skills! Through this project the children can develop ICT capability while participating in the creation of their own concept cartoon.

Activity 1: Introducing concept cartoons

If this is the children's first introduction to concept cartoons, then introducing the topic using a file like the one below on the interactive whiteboard is a good idea. It will help if the actual apparatus, or a model, is available too – in this instance two containers of soup.

Through questioning, discussion and adding text using the whiteboard software, some of the children's current understanding can be elicited and their ideas can be recorded on the screen. While it is possible to include a word bank at this stage, you may want to start from the children's own words and build a word bank as the project develops. There are several examples available from the ASE and cartoons can be created for almost any age and to address learning in most areas of science.

A concept cartoon created using Textease

Activity 2: Making a cartoon

The children use a range of word-processing and formatting tools to present and communicate their understanding of scientific concepts by completing or creating their own cartoon. The activity can be easily differentiated by handing over different amounts of the task for the children to complete. At one end of the scale the children could type their viewpoint into the prepared speech bubble; at the other, they could draw or photograph the scene and create their own cartoon entirely, making the speech bubbles or thought balloons and adding the text.

What should the children know already?

It is possible to complete a concept cartoon as a class or group activity without needing or developing any ICT capability. Depending on the prior experience and capability of the children, appropriate parts of this activity can be used as the focus of their ICT development. It could, for example, focus solely on working with word banks, or creating and grouping drawing elements to add speech bubbles to an existing cartoon.

How to input text

Some knowledge of the keyboard will enable the activity to be completed independently, but, due to the small amount of text needed for the dialogue bubbles, this is an appropriate activity for keyboard novices.

How to select objects – in this case words from a word bank – by moving the mouse and clicking

If a word bank is to be used, words are normally inserted by pointing at the word required and clicking. The insertion of Clip Art and drawing objects will also require the selection and dragging of selected items.

What do I need to know?

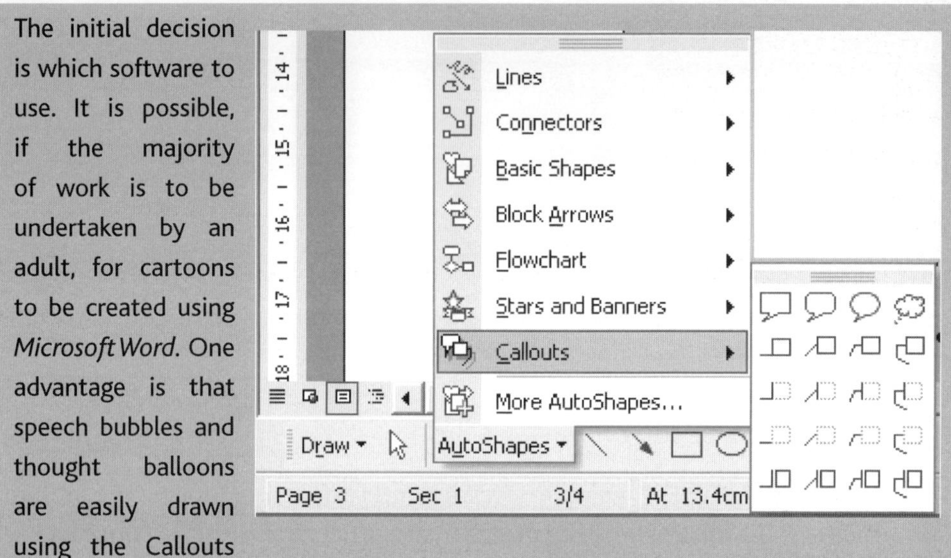

The initial decision is which software to use. It is possible, if the majority of work is to be undertaken by an adult, for cartoons to be created using *Microsoft Word*. One advantage is that speech bubbles and thought balloons are easily drawn using the Callouts Autoshapes available on the **Drawing** toolbar.

If the **Drawing** toolbar is not visible at the bottom of the page when you open *Microsoft Word*, select **Toolbars** > **Drawing** from the **View** menu and it should be revealed.

Children can still add text to the cartoon and the file can still be used on the interactive whiteboard. For the children to be more involved in the creation of the cartoon and for access to word banks, however, a more appropriate infant word processor like *Textease* from Softease or RM *Talking First Word* will be required. The example here will refer to *Word* and *Textease*.

How to insert pictures into a word-processed document

The essential element of a cartoon is a graphic image and there is a variety of sources for the images to be inserted into your cartoon:

- Clip Art available in the software or from CD-ROMs or the internet
- Digital photographs – again either from your own camera, the internet or Photo CD-ROMs
- Digital artwork – drawings created using *Paint* software
- Children's artwork completed using conventional media and scanned

Once the image exists in electronic format as a computer file it can be inserted into a *Word* document by selecting **Picture > From File . . .** from the **Insert** menu and navigating to the folder where the file is stored. When the picture appears it is inserted 'in line' with the text – that is, it becomes like a character or letter which can be positioned across the page by inserting spaces before it. In order to be able to position the picture by dragging it, the picture needs to be reformatted. Select the picture and then choose **Picture . . .** from the **Format** menu.

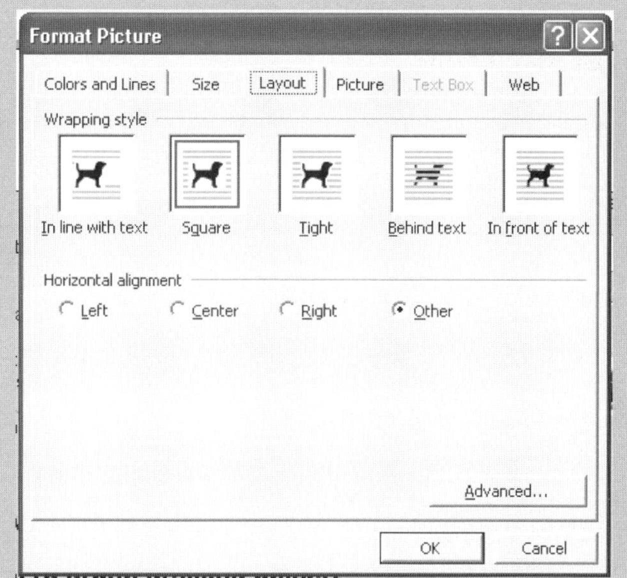

In the dialogue box choose the **Layout** tab at the top and select **Square**. When you click **OK** the picture should be able to be moved by clicking and dragging.

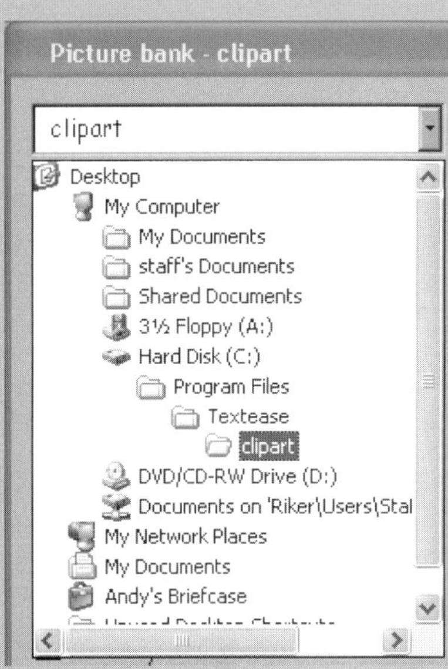

In *Textease*, access to quite a wide range of Clip Art and graphic resources is available by clicking on the **Picture bank** icon. A list of folders containing Clip Art and photographs sorted by category will appear on the right-hand side of the screen. Clicking on a folder name will open the folder to display 'thumbnails' or small versions of the Clip Art. To insert an image simply click on it and drag it to position it on the page. *Textease* automatically opens the Clip Art folder which is supplied with the program but it is possible to navigate to other folders – a CD-ROM collection, for example – by clicking on the drop-down arrow at the top of the Clip Art window.

How to use simple draw tools to create speech bubbles

The speech bubbles and thought balloons available in *Microsoft Word* do not come as standard with all drawing or word-processing software. They are quite easy to recreate using circle and line tools or even freehand. First draw an ellipse by stretching out a circle using the circle tool. Then draw a triangle using the polygon or free-form tool. Most software has a tool of this sort which allows irregular shapes to be created – a little like making a rubber band shape; each click of the mouse nails the line and straight lines are drawn between the mouse clicks.

While the shape is still selected use the drawing tools or effects window in *Textease* – which is accessed by clicking on the large red 'e' on the toolbar – to remove the line around the shape or to colour it the same as the fill colour. The two shapes can then be positioned side by side without appearing to be separate. It will be apparent that the speech bubble is made of separate elements when any attempt is made to move it on the screen. It is therefore useful to be able to connect the two elements together so that they will move as a single element or group.

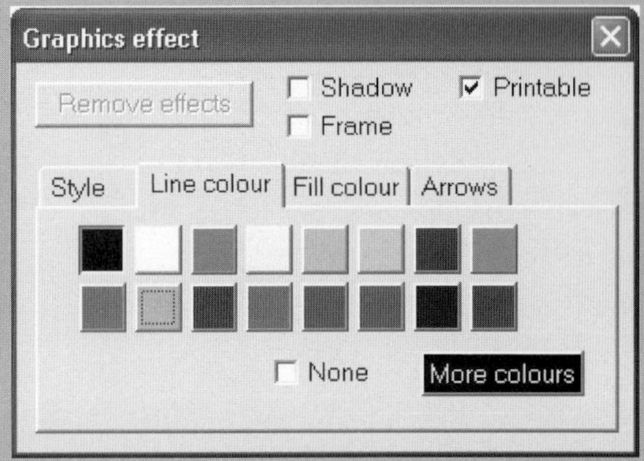

How to group drawing objects

The majority of drawing software will enable elements drawn separately to be grouped together. The two, or more, shapes that are to be combined must first be drawn and selected. This can be a problem as selecting an object usually de-selects anything previously selected. In some software holding down the SHIFT (⇧) key while multiple selections are made will enable several objects to be selected. In *Textease* it is the **Ctrl** (Control) key that needs to be held down while the second and subsequent objects are selected or clicking and dragging diagonally across a collection of shapes will select them all. It is clear to see which shapes have been selected as they will all have 'handles' visible around them.

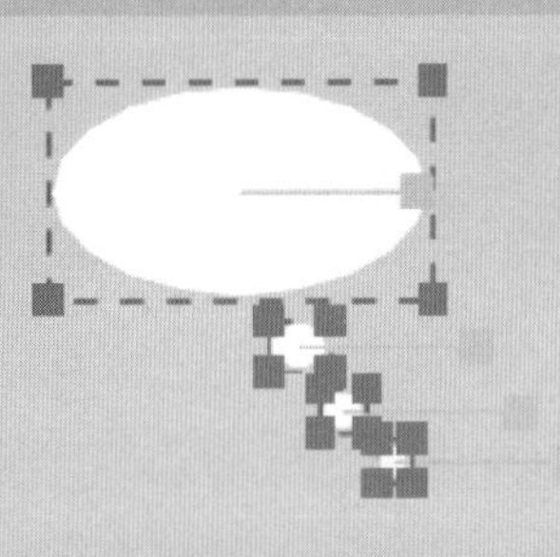

While the objects are selected in this way, click on the **Group** tool on the toolbar. The multiple 'handles' will then disappear to be replaced by a single set enabling the group to be resized or repositioned easily.

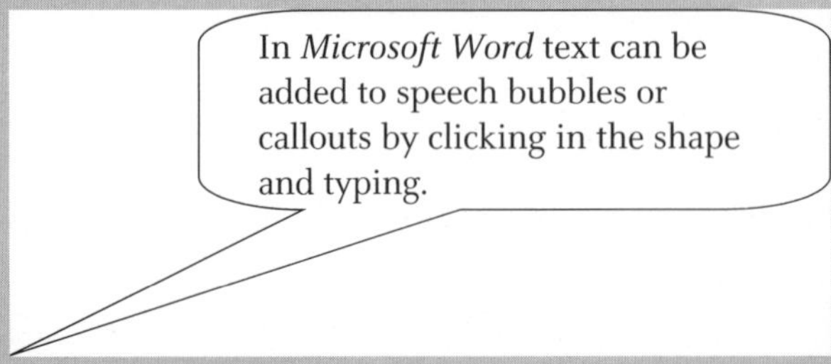

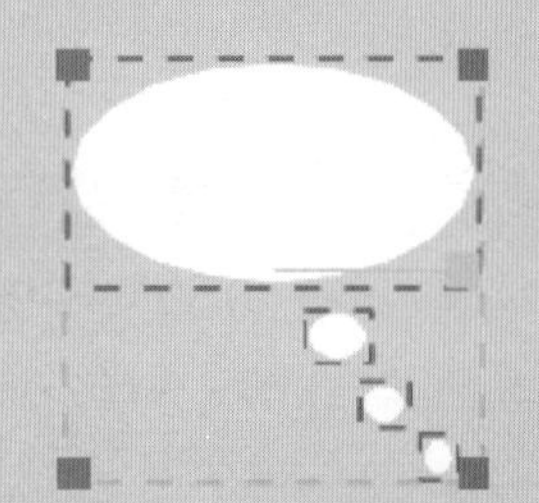

How to order drawing objects one behind the other

Drawing software can be thought to consist of several layers of acetate. Each time an object is drawn it is assigned a layer; it is possible to make objects appear to be in front of others by bringing them forward or sending other objects backwards. In *Microsoft Word* this can be achieved by selecting **Order** from the **Draw** menu on the **Drawing** toolbar when the object is selected. In *Textease* the object that needs to be raised or lowered in the order also needs to be selected. It can then be moved by selecting **Higher** or **Lower** from the **Tools** menu or holding down the **Ctrl** key and pressing **L** or **H**.

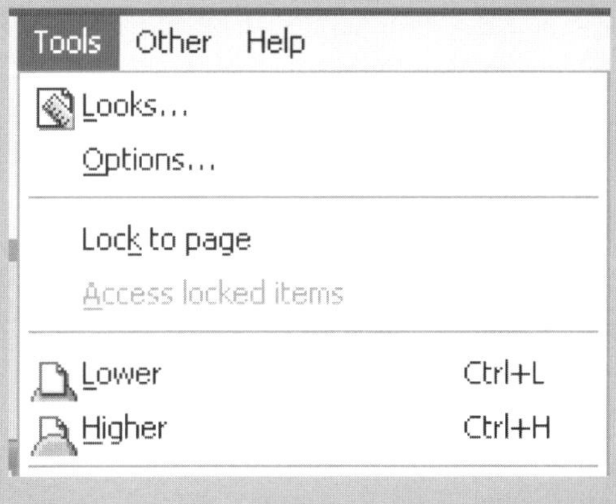

How to create text boxes

In some software it is necessary to add a text box if you wish to have text appear inside a shape like speech bubbles. Normally in *Textease* it is possible to click anywhere on the page and begin to type. With a filled shape, however, it will be necessary to place a text box over the ellipse so that speech or thoughts can be added.

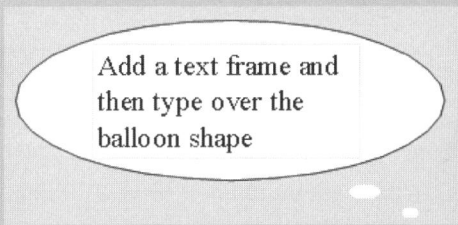

Add a text frame and then type over the balloon shape

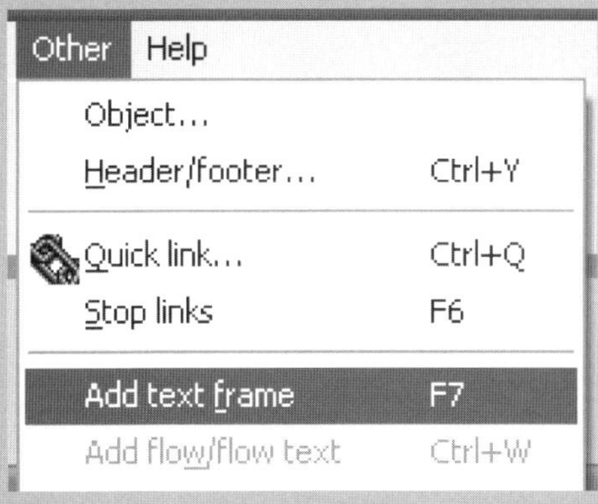

First select **Add text frame** from the *Textease* **Other** menu and then click and drag to create the frame over the speech bubble.

Click inside the frame and type to add a caption. The text frame can be grouped with the balloon shape by selecting both in the way described above.

How to set up a word bank

A word bank can be a very effective way to support children's learning in science. By aiding the children's literacy skills and providing the appropriate technical vocabulary the focus of the activity can remain with the concept at the heart of the cartoon. *Textease* word banks can be typed quickly and, when a word is clicked on, it will be transferred from the word bank to the speech bubble – or wherever the cursor is – automatically. An added advantage for early readers is that clicking on the word with the right button – i.e. not left! – of the mouse will cause the software to speak the word.

Using a word bank in Textease

To create a word bank to accompany a concept cartoon it is important to do it collaboratively with the children so that the words that they want to use to describe their point of view are included alongside the vocabulary that you may wish to introduce.

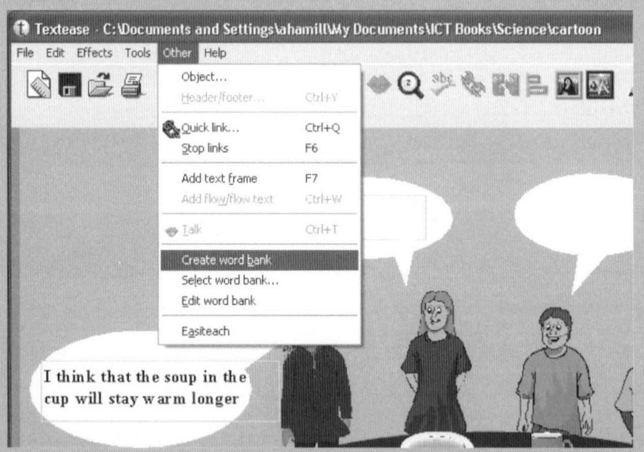

With the cartoon file open, select **Create word bank** from the **Other** menu. A new narrow window will appear and the list can be typed pressing **RETURN** or **ENTER** (↵) after each word. The text can be formatted by using the effects tools.

Once complete the word bank needs to be saved and then clicking on the **Word** bank icon will activate the list so that the words change colour as you roll the mouse over them and they can be spoken or inserted in the manner described above.

How to use the interactive whiteboard to add text

Whether or not there is access to an interactive whiteboard, the concept cartoon file can be used with the whole class. It is possible to record children's ideas by using a volunteer to operate the computer either directly or via a wireless keyboard. If an interactive whiteboard is available, then text can be entered using either the handwriting-recognition facility or the electronic marker pen available in most whiteboard software. The whiteboard software operates over the top of the *Textease* file, enabling 'electronic annotation'. *Easiteach* calls this 'glass mode' so that any writing added behaves as if it is being added to a sheet of glass in front of the file. Children can be encouraged to use the drawing tool to write on the screen and although their writing is not being added to the *Textease* file it is possible to use the camera snapshot tool to save a record of the children's ideas for assessment purposes.

A *Textease* file containing an example of a concept cartoon is provided on the CD-ROM accompanying this book, to enable you to experiment, or to demonstrate to the children.

What will the children learn?

That ICT can be used to create pictures to present information

Irrespective of how much or little the children contribute to the creation of the cartoon, they will learn about the possibilities if we talk about the process. Particularly as children progress to National Curriculum assessment, talking about uses of ICT becomes important. Make the most of opportunities to model the use of ICT by making adjustments to the cartoon, changing the position or size of one of the characters, for instance, while the children are watching.

To use ICT appropriately to communicate ideas through text and images

The limited amount of text and familiarity of the cartoon genre makes this an attractive way for young learners to communicate their ideas. There are many opportunities to extend children's understanding of ICT and develop their skills to be able to appropriate use of it.

That ICT makes it easy to correct mistakes and explore alternatives

As this task is about exploring children's views and helping to clarify their thinking, the provisional nature of the medium, which enables them to revise and alter the text that they add to the speech balloons, is of genuine value.

That computers use icons to provide information and instructions

Even if children do not use the icons there are many opportunities to model their use or involve the children in a group activity – helping to look for the appropriate icon to draw a circle, for example.

Challenging the more able and supporting the less able: modifying the project for older and younger pupils

While it is possible to use this ICT resource as a focus for discussion and to support the children who struggle with the technology, the purpose is that the activity is developmental for all children in terms of both their ICT capability and their science knowledge and understanding. As with all good teaching, the key is to identify the next step that the children can cope with. It is important that we consider their ICT and science needs separately. It does not necessarily follow that a child who is finding the scientific concept challenging will need support with ICT tasks. It goes without saying that the larger science topic of which this activity forms a part should provide the children with opportunities to investigate the concept at first hand. Depending on the needs of the children, providing software that supports word banks and creating a bank of vocabulary or typing ideas for them may help. Using children's drawings as a part of the cartoon, even if the scanning and insertion of the images is carried out by an adult, will develop their understanding of the capabilities of the technology and provide a valuable focus for discussion.

It should be evident from the steps involved in the creation of this resource, outlined above, that there is a wealth of opportunity to involve children in any of the stages of the creation of the cartoon – even helping to create a word bank. By looking at the needs of the able children appropriate challenges can be found to develop their ICT capability, ensuring that they save, retrieve and amend their work and that they are given opportunities to explore the effects of alternatives to both the text and the layout of the cartoon. Some children may be able to make their own drawings either using *Paint* software or scanning in original artwork before adding the dialogue in the software. It is also possible to create a tableau of the cartoon – a group of children gathered around an investigation, for example – and take a digital photograph. The thoughts and contributions of the children can then be added to the photograph using the software.

Why teach this?

The exploratory nature of wrestling with a scientific concept makes ICT a natural choice of tool to assist with the completion of concept cartoons. The real-life context provided by the cartoon's scenario also brings a purpose to the development of ICT skills. Thus, as well as contributing to NC ICT, these activities promote and explore children's understanding of science. Depending upon the extent to which the children become involved in the creation of the cartoon, different elements of the ICT KS1 PoS will be addressed. All children will experience the use of ICT to exchange and share information (3a), and the creation of a cartoon either by assembling Clip Art, creating drawings or taking and using photographs will contribute to the development of ideas (2a, 2d).

This project offers a context for QCA ICT Scheme of Work Unit 1B: *Using a word bank*. It is also possible, by involving the children in the creation of the cartoon, to cover the key ideas introduced in Unit 2B: *Creating pictures*:

- That ICT can be used to create pictures
- That ICT makes it easy to correct mistakes and explore alternatives
- To select and use different techniques to communicate ideas through pictures

QCA Unit 3A: *Combining text and graphics* introduces font type, size and colour for emphasis and effect and the use of the **SHIFT** key to type characters, such as question marks, which could easily be included in the activity.

Concept cartoons by their nature deal with the science NC Attainment Targets (ATs) 2–4. As well as the area of science knowledge which is the focus of the cartoon, the project also contributes to Science NC KS1 PoS statements Sc1, 2g, using ICT to communicate, and 2i, as they explain their expectations. It is possible to design an appropriate concept cartoon activity of this sort for any of the QCA Science Scheme of Work units for Key Stage 1.

See also *English* Project 7 (*Photo-dramas*) for related activities.

Project Fact Card: Project 4: Branching databases

Who is it for?

- 6- to 7-year-olds (NC Levels 1–3)

What will the children do?

- Sort collections of materials by careful observation of their properties and create a key using branching database software. Use other children's keys to identify materials

What should the children know already?

- How to select items on the screen
- How to enter text
- How to use simple draw tools

What do I need to know?

- The difference between branching and flat file databases
- How to create branching data files of different sizes
- How to frame and enter a sorting question
- How to specify folders to save to
- How to interrogate a branching data file

What resources will I need?

- Branching database software

What will the children learn?

- That a tree diagram can be used to organise information and that a branching database can be used to store and sort information which can be searched
- That objects can be divided according to criteria and that collecting and storing information in an organised way helps them find answers to questions
- How to prepare data for a database; that some questions have only yes/no answers and have to be phrased carefully
- That a database can only answer questions if appropriate data have been entered

How to challenge the more able

- Provide information sources for children to name the items in the collection
- Work with a group of similar objects so that differences are less pronounced
- Work with a larger group of objects to create a larger data file

How to support the less able

- Help to develop a vocabulary to name and classify objects
- Work with objects with clearly recognised differences
- Work with a smaller group of objects to create a smaller data file

Why teach this?

- The project is targeted at section 1 of the ICT NC KS1 PoS, 'Finding things out'. It adds an important dimension also to the breadth of study in the type of information, the specific use of database tools and the chance to consider the use of databases outside school.
- The project augments and extends the content of QCA ICT Scheme of Work Units 1C and 1D. It also provides a simplified introduction to Units 3C and 4C in KS2.
- The grouping and classification of materials and animals is a key part of the Science National Curriculum Sc2 and Sc3. The use of ICT is also part of the requirements for Sc1 and a deeper understanding of ICT-based sources, afforded by the creation of a simple branching database, will help to address the use of ICT sources described in the 'Breadth of study'. Any first-hand observations will benefit from a more detailed and disciplined classification exercise which the use of this type of software demands. Opportunities exist in the QCA Science Scheme of Work Units 1A, 1B, 1C, 2C and 2D.

PROJECT 4

Branching databases

What will the children do?

Sorting is a fundamental activity for young learners. This activity begins to take children from sorting to classifying and naming objects, materials or creatures based on their characteristics and properties. Guessing games such as 'I am thinking of an animal with . . .' or 'My flower has . . .', using a real collection of objects that the children can sort, are needed before the children embark on the ICT tasks. There are two aspects of the ICT work for this project: the creation and the interrogation of a branching database. The two parts are necessary for the children to see that the computer is asking precisely the questions that the children have typed in. The creation of the branching database may be completed over several sessions and, similarly, the resulting files may be interrogated on numerous occasions.

Activity 1: Getting sorted

Once the children are familiar with the collection of objects that they are studying they can begin to work on devising and recording the questions that will divide the group ultimately, step by step, until each object is identified. There are several software titles designed for the creation of branching data files by primary-aged children. Some are more sophisticated and complex than others. The *2question* software from the *2Simple Infant Video Toolkit* works with a simple tree structure so the collections of 4, 8 or 16 objects need to be carefully selected by the teacher to ensure that they will divide in two at each partitioning of the set. At each stage the children can represent the question in

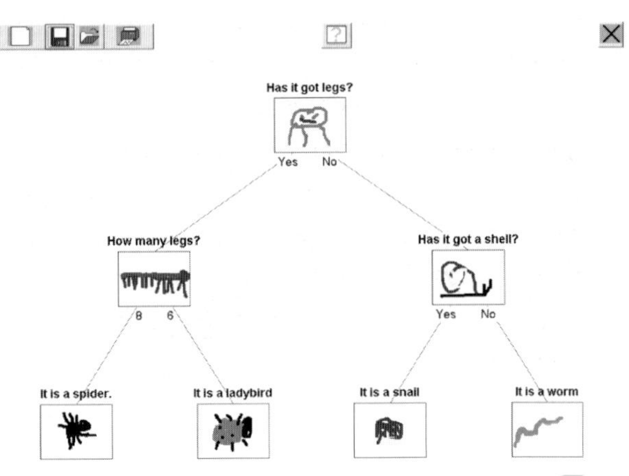

both words and a simple drawing using paint brush tools. Software like *ReTreeval* (Kudlian Soft), for example, allows uneven partitioning of sets.

A *ReTreeval* handbook is provided on the CD-ROM accompanying this book.

Activity 2: What am I?

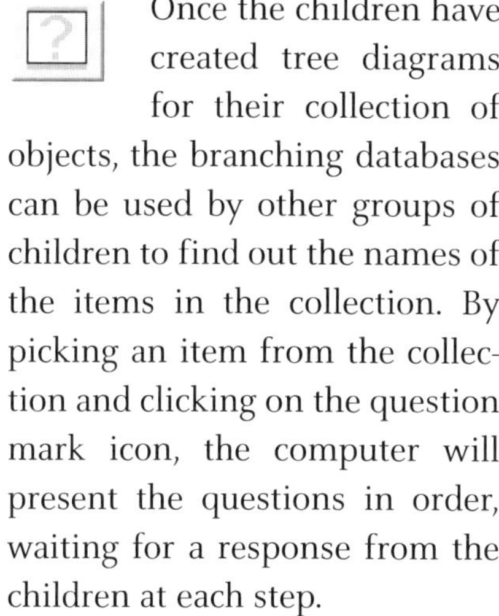

Once the children have created tree diagrams for their collection of objects, the branching databases can be used by other groups of children to find out the names of the items in the collection. By picking an item from the collection and clicking on the question mark icon, the computer will present the questions in order, waiting for a response from the children at each step.

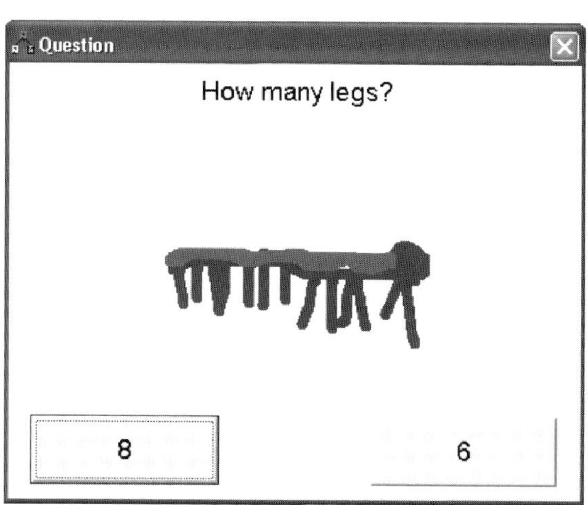

What should the children know already?

The linguistic and scientific content of this activity is more demanding than the ICT skills required at the outset. While it will help the children to focus on the key learning about databases if they are familiar with **how to select items on the screen**, **how to enter text** and **how to use simple draw tools**, it is possible for them to undertake the tasks outlined above with limited previous experience.

What do I need to know?

The difference between branching and flat file databases

While the terms are not helpful for young children, it is useful for those teaching to understand the structure and limitations of different types of software. A flat file database is a simple database system in which each database is contained in a single table with each record making up one line of the table. A phone directory would be a simple example with each person's entry being a record. The columns of the table are known as the fields – in the phone book they would be *Name: Address: Phone number*. In the branching database the location of the record is significant as the information about the record is described by its pathway; for example, *has legs – no, and has a shell – yes.*

How to create branching data files of different sizes

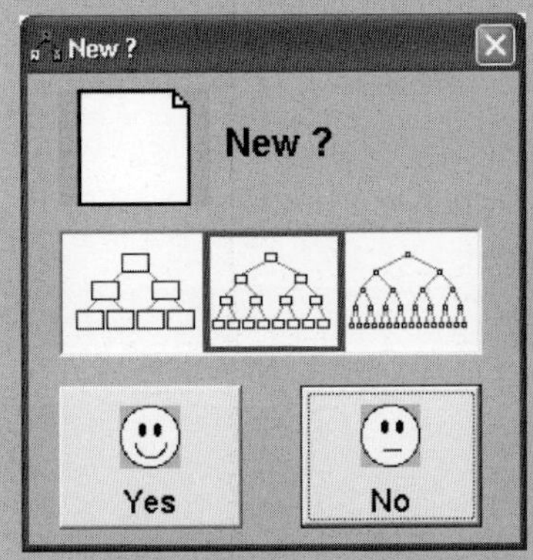

Some branching database software will let you add records to the database and adjust the structure to accommodate it. The *2simple* software requires you to select the size of the set that you are going to work with from a choice of three. When you first launch *2question* select the new icon to create a new database. A dialogue box will appear to invite you to choose from three sizes of tree diagram. The smallest enables four items to be classified by constructing three sorting questions; the largest can record a set of sixteen items and requires the construction of fifteen sorting questions. Click **Yes** once you have made your selection and a new blank file of the size that you have specified will be created.

How to frame and enter a sorting question

It is important not to underestimate the complexity of framing sorting questions. The first example needs to be constructed collaboratively with the children. Using the collection of materials play some sorting games where you partition the set in two equal amounts using a criterion (shiny materials, for example) and invite the children to identify the reason for your selection. Once they have explained the criterion – 'They are all shiny' – the statement needs to be turned into a question that has two possible answers only, usually 'Yes' or 'No'. So 'Is it shiny?' will produce the answer 'No' for half of the objects and 'Yes' for the other half. The question and answer are entered in the tree diagram by clicking on the rectangular box at the top of the diagram. When the **Edit Question** box appears, the question can be typed at the top and the two possible answers typed in the boxes at the bottom. Simple coloured pen icons allow a picture to be added. Clicking on **OK** will transfer the information to the diagram. Each subset of articles is dealt with in the same way, working your way down the page following each branch of the diagram so that ultimately each individual item is identified.

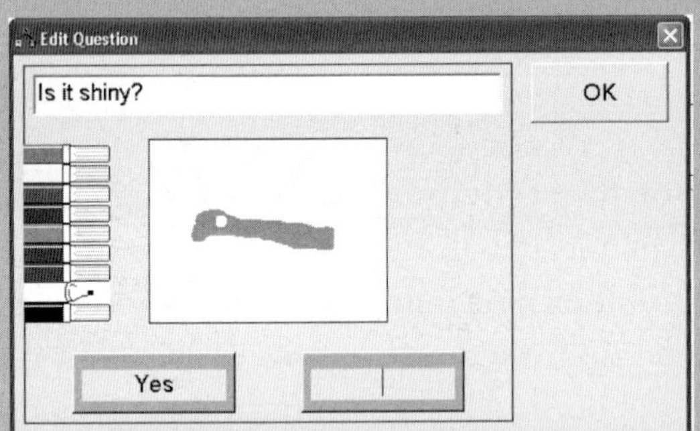

The bottom layer of boxes needs to identify what the object is so that when the key is used the computer will be able to identify the object based on the answers that

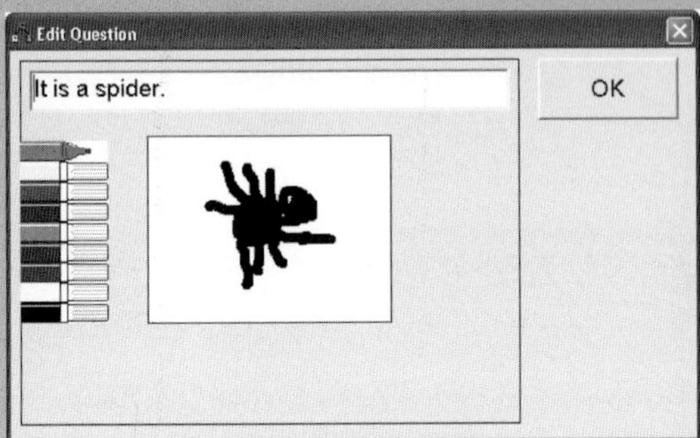

the children have given. With the diagram complete, the file needs to be saved before the file is tested and used by others; it is a good idea to save the file and give it a name at the beginning so that work may be recovered in the event of a failure of the system.

How to specify folders to save to

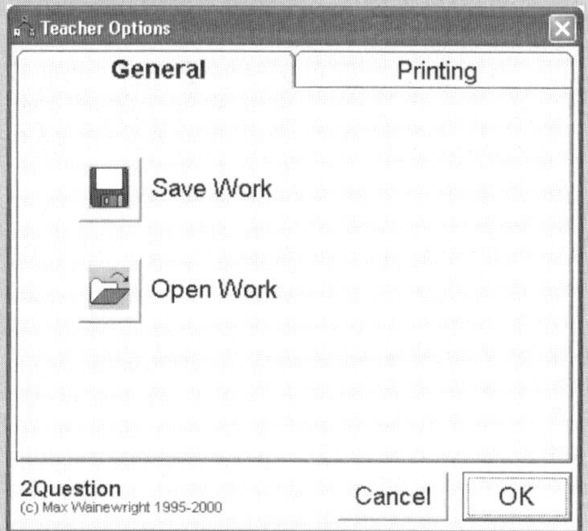

As simple infant software, *2question* only allows files to be saved in a designated folder. It is possible to alter the folder by accessing the teacher options. With the software running hold down **SHIFT** and **Ctrl** keys at the same time and simultaneously press the **o** key. The **Teacher options** box appears where saving and opening folders can be selected and also printers chosen. To change the **Save Work** folder click on the icon and then navigate to the folder that you want the children's work to be saved in; name the current file and click **OK**. Close the **Teacher options** box. The next time the save icon is clicked the selected folder will be opened.

How to interrogate a branching data file

Once a complete file has been created and saved it can be opened and used as a key for other children to name the objects that have been classified in the branching database. Open the file and click on the [?] icon. An object is selected from the collection and the children answer the questions on the screen for the object that they have chosen.

The questions that the children have entered will be presented in turn by the computer. The sequence of questions will depend on the answers given by the group using the database. If the questions have been entered and answered correctly the data file should name the object that they have selected.

What will the children learn?

That a tree diagram can be used to organise information and that a branching database can be used to store and sort information which can be searched

That the children use the branching data files as well as create them is a necessary part of the learning in this project. Valuable learning can ensue when the children debate disputed characteristics or ambiguity in questions. The questions are easily edited by clicking on the diagram so the children can be helped to improve their work.

That objects can be divided according to criteria and that collecting and storing information in an organised way helps them find answers to questions

When properly constructed, the children's data files are able to identify and name objects. The visual representation of their sorting also helps to reveal the process of classifying that the children have 'taught' the computer.

How to prepare data for a database; that some questions have only yes/no answers and have to be phrased carefully

It would be naïve to think that all children will be able to phrase these sorting questions independently, but by interrogating the information too, the importance of clear questions and preparing the sorting carefully will become apparent.

That a database can only answer questions if appropriate data have been entered

The value of the computer as an obedient servant that will answer precisely as it has been taught is part of the attraction to young learners. Knowing that the accuracy of the file is dependent on the information that has been entered brings a sharpened purpose to the activity and added depth to the learning.

Challenging the more able and supporting the less able: modifying the project for older and younger pupils

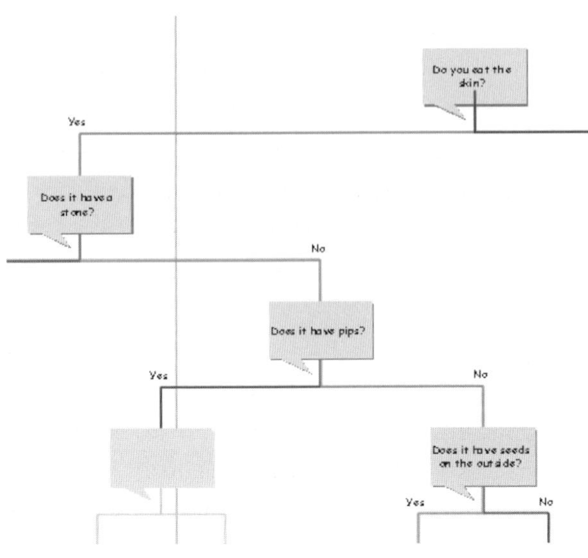

With suitable degrees of support all children can participate in the recording of information in this type of branching database. If reading is an issue, *Textease Branch* is a more sophisticated branching database which makes use of the speech facility to read questions out to children. As they click on the appropriate 'Yes' or 'No' response the next question is revealed and read out to the children.

While *Textease Branch* software will create more complex trees it has several support facilities which can assist young learners with the creation of branching data files by dragging words or pictures of your chosen collection of objects to sort them according to the questions that they type. It also provides help via sound files which give spoken instructions to explain what to do at each step. The creation of the questions helps children to develop a vocabulary to name and classify the objects. If some children have difficulty describing the objects, more sorting games playing with the collection will help to introduce the necessary vocabulary.

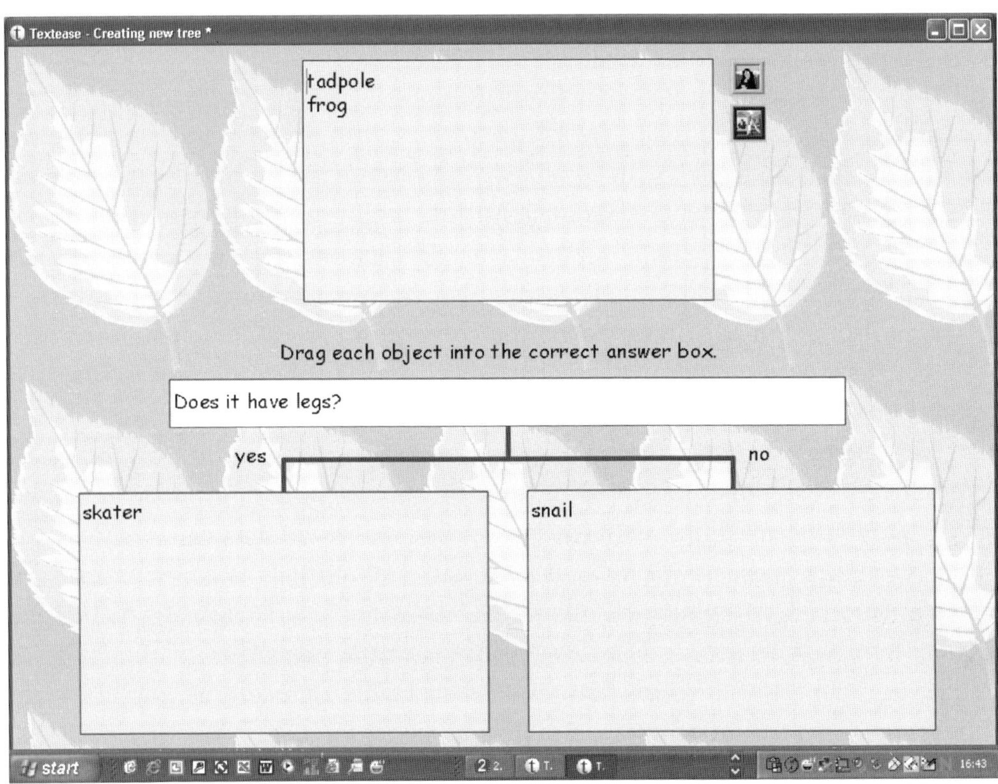

Creating a tree using Textease Branch

For some children subtle distinctions between similar objects may prove challenging. By working with objects with clearly recognised differences the framing of questions can be supported. Similarly, limiting the number of objects will reduce the task and lead to the creation a smaller data file. It is worth noting that reducing a task that children find difficult is not always helpful to their development as it is precisely the tasks that they find difficult that may need further practice.

To extend the capable children and add further dimensions to the task in both science and ICT, information sources for children to name the items in the collection could be provided. Using information sources of any kind to find things out is an important aspect of the science curriculum; using online or CD-ROM-based sources contributes to both the science and the ICT curricula.

Those children whose observation skills are already well developed may be able to work with a group of similar objects so that differences are less pronounced and sharper examination of the items will be required. The subtle differences will also challenge the children's vocabulary as the sorting questions will need to be precise.

While a larger group of objects will certainly be more demanding as a larger data file will need to be created, it is important that by increasing the set of objects, the task remains genuinely developmental and challenging for the needs of the children, not merely repetitive because of the quantity of items.

Why teach this?

The projected activity is targeted at section 1 of the ICT NC KS1 PoS, 'Finding things out'. It adds an important dimension also to the breadth of study in several ways. First, activities of this sort add to the range of information that the children will have processed using ICT. Whatever the specific science focus of the project, the children should have the opportunity to work with primary sources and classify the information in a way that enables others to use it. The specific use of database tools will add a valuable dimension to the children's understanding of the capability of the software; and the chance to consider the use of databases outside school, as well as addressing the PoS, provides useful assessment opportunities.

The project augments and extends the content of QCA ICT Scheme of Work Unit 1C: *The information around us* and adds an additional dimension to Unit 1D: *Labelling and classifying.* It also could provide a simplified introduction to Units 3C: *Introduction to databases* and 4C: *Branching databases* in Key Stage 2. Alternatively it is possible to use more sophisticated software and extend the science content to make this activity appropriate for Key Stage 2.

The grouping and classification of materials and animals is a key part of the Science National Curriculum activity in this Sc2 and Sc3. This project would make a purposeful task in the study of living things or the properties of materials. A branching database of the birds that visit the bird table, for example, would enable children to name the different species by answering a series of Yes/No questions. The use of ICT is also part of the requirements for Sc1, and a deeper understanding of ICT-based sources, afforded by the creation of a simple branching database, will help to address the use of ICT sources described in the 'Breadth of study'. The first-hand observations that the children make will benefit from the more detailed and disciplined classification exercise which the use of this type of software demands. As a branching database is constructed, the children have to observe more and more closely as they try to find differences between items that are similar. Opportunities exist to adapt this project to suit the content of several of the KS1 QCA Scheme of Work units, including 1A: *Ourselves,* 1B: *Growing plants,* 1C: *Sorting and using materials,* 2C: *Variation* and 2D: *Grouping and changing materials.*

See also *Humanities* Project 6 (*Using a database to analyse census data*), *Arts* Project 7 (*Using a spreadsheet model*), *English* Project 3 (*Branching stories*) and *Maths* Project 6 (*Statistical investigations 1*) for related activities.

Project Fact Card: Project 5: Graphical representation of data

Who is it for?

- 7- to 8-year-olds (NC Levels 2–4)

What will the children do?

- The children will use a ready-prepared spreadsheet file to enter and analyse data collected from an investigation. Using the graph facility of the spreadsheet software a graph of their findings will be generated so that the children can focus on using their scientific knowledge to explain the data

What should the children know already?

- Where to insert text and enter numbers
- The function of the **Delete** (Del) and **Back Space** (←) keys
- The principles of saving and printing work will help to prepare them for the spreadsheet if it is a new piece of software for them

What do I need to know?

- The difference between discrete and continuous data
- How to create and format a table in a spreadsheet
- How to select data in a spreadsheet and create a graph
- How to format a graph
- How to lock parts of a spreadsheet
- How to make a 'Read-only' file
- How to transfer a graph to a word processor

What resources will I need?

- Spreadsheet software such as *Microsoft Excel, Softease* or BlackCat *NumberBox 2*
- Word-processing software such as *Microsoft Word* or *Granada Writer v3*

What will the children learn?

- To use ICT to enter data in a spreadsheet and present findings
- That data represented graphically can be easier to understand than textual data
- That information represented as graphs can be interpreted and analysed to provide answers to questions
- That information comes from a variety of sources and can be presented in a variety of forms
- To identify and correct implausible and inaccurate data
- That ICT can be used for collecting, storing and sorting information in an organised way

How to challenge the more able

- Hand over elements of the creation of the spreadsheet to more able children, e.g. selecting the type of graph that will best display the data
- Ensure that they save and amend the data
- Encourage them to compare the spreadsheet task with their own graph drawing

How to support the less able

- Read their results to them while they enter data
- Discuss the way that the spreadsheet was prepared
- Draw the children's attention to the graph-making function of the spreadsheet
- Explain the layout of the table carefully
- Help to explain and analyse the graph

Why teach this?

- ICT makes an important contribution to scientific research at all levels. The focus of this project is section 1 of the ICT NC KS2 PoS, 'Finding things out'. The children gather, store and retrieve information. They are also expected to address section 3, 'Exchanging and sharing information', as they present the findings of their investigations.
- The project builds on the content of QCA ICT Scheme of Work Units 1E and 2E. It develops similar ICT skills as Unit 3A and complements Unit 4D. It also provides a useful link to Units 5B and 5C.
- The project supports Science NC KS2 PoS statements Sc1, particularly 2f–l and can be applied to any investigation where numerical data are collected in the QCA scheme of work units for science.

PROJECT 5

Graphical representation of data

What will the children do?

With minor amendments this activity can be used to support almost any scientific investigation where the graphical representation of numerical data will support children's analysis of their findings. This use of ICT is a form of scaffolding where, in this instance, the construction of graphs is being supported by the technology to enable children to focus on what the numbers actually tell us in scientific terms. Even if the children do little more than enter numbers and print out their graph, by discussing the role of ICT we can make sure that the activity develops children's knowledge and understanding of ICT.

Activity 1: Entering data

Using a prepared spreadsheet the children enter their experimental data which is turned into a graph by the software. Because of the way that the spreadsheet file is prepared, the graph is automatically generated as the numbers are typed in to the table – in this instance the results of measuring the length of shadow of a stick in the ground at half-hour intervals during the day.

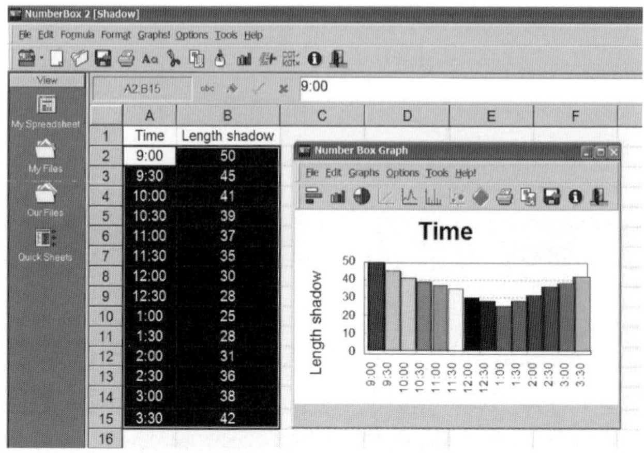

A prepared spreadsheet using BlackCat NumberBox 2

The graph can then be printed out for children to discuss or used in a word-processed report.

Activity 2: Exploring data

For children who are capable it helps to make sure that they save the spreadsheet file and come back to amend the data. Some children may also adapt the spreadsheet to explore other types of graph or extend or modify it to compare additional data.

What should the children know already?

Where to insert text and enter numbers

The children should be confident with selecting where to insert text and enter numbers. The need to position the cursor in the correct cell or rectangular box on the spreadsheet before they type is important. In this case, reminding them of the need to record results in the box next door to the time that the measurement was made will help.

The function of the Delete (Del) and Back Space (←) keys

Normally, in a word processor, the **Back Space** key will delete the character on the left of the cursor position and the **Delete** key will delete the character to the right. The contents of a selected cell in most spreadsheet software will be deleted with either key. When double clicking on a cell to edit its contents or editing on the **Formula** bar at the top of an *Excel* sheet, the keys behave as they would in a word processor.

The principles of saving and printing work will help to prepare them for the spreadsheet if it is a new piece of software for them

Previous experience with saving files will help children, as nearly all software has the **Save As . . .** and **Print** commands in the **File** menu if they do not have separate icons on the toolbar. Saving work at the start is a good habit to adopt to avoid losing data, whether or not there is a plan to use the spreadsheet again. It also keeps open the option to revisit and amend data at a later stage.

What do I need to know?

The example spreadsheet files used in this section and a 'Handling Data' booklet are available on the CD-ROM accompanying this book.

The difference between discrete and continuous data

Why does it matter? If we are going to represent data graphically, then the graphs must make sense. In the example of measuring shadow length it could have been possible to represent the data as a line graph as it is reasonable that had we gone out to measure the shadows at more frequent intervals we would have found a length of shadow somewhere between the two measurements as the shadow length is changing continuously, not in discrete steps.

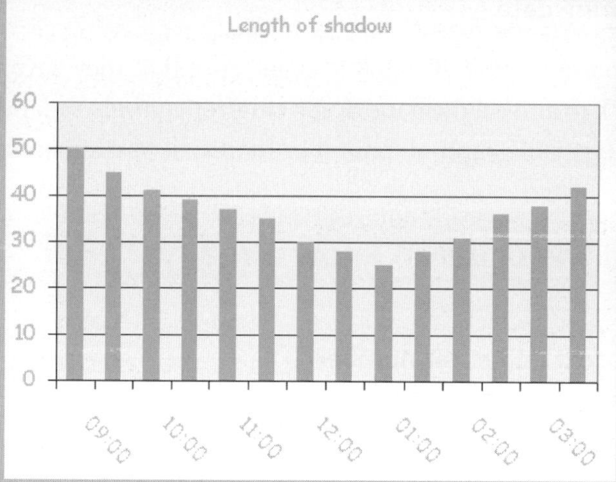

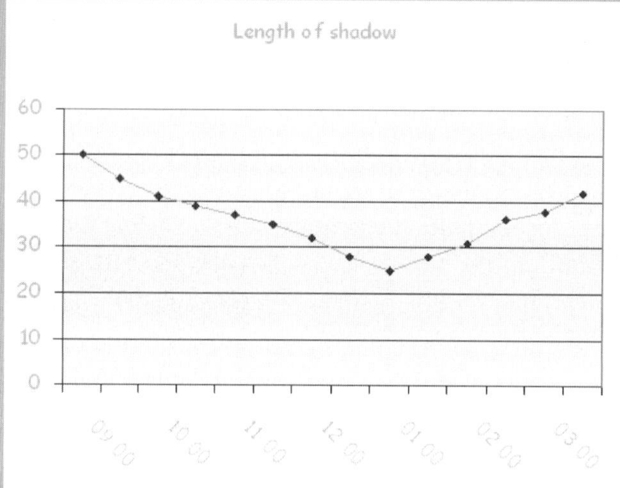

If, on the other hand, we were recording the number of birds feeding on the bird-table each half-hour through the day, we could not assume that just because there were 6 at half-past nine and 8 at ten o'clock that there would have been 7 at quarter to ten. The line in between the two records does not make sense so a bar chart would be more appropriate. The danger with spreadsheet software is that the very professional chart which the software produces can be assumed to be correct and accurate but only reflects the accuracy of the data and the choices made by the operator.

How to create and format a table in a spreadsheet

A spreadsheet is a tool for accountants designed to deal with tables of numbers and perform mathematical operations upon them. Spreadsheets will also generate graphs from tables of figures if they are correctly entered. When a new spreadsheet file is opened a grid of rows and columns will be revealed. Each rectangle in the grid is called a 'cell' and is uniquely identifiable by its column letter and row number – A2 or F9. *Excel* is the Microsoft spreadsheet and there are primary spreadsheets which behave in a very similar way such as the *Softease Spreadsheet* or BlackCat *NumberBox 2*.

Any of these can be used for this project and the tasks will be explained where they function differently.

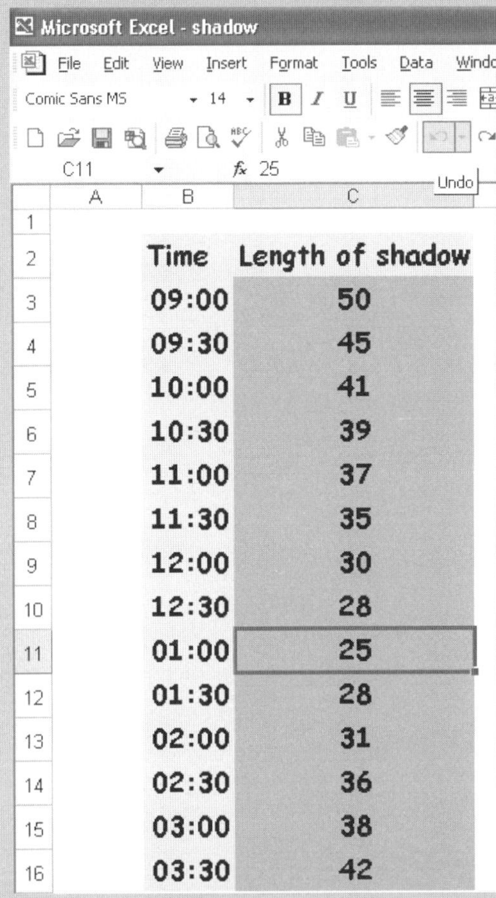

	A	B	C
1			
2		Time	Length of shadow
3		09:00	50
4		09:30	45
5		10:00	41
6		10:30	39
7		11:00	37
8		11:30	35
9		12:00	30
10		12:30	28
11		01:00	25
12		01:30	28
13		02:00	31
14		02:30	36
15		03:00	38
16		03:30	42

First of all click in each cell in turn and type the text or numbers. The headings are important as they will be used later to label the graph. Although the results are going to be added later by the children, it helps to create some fictitious data to test that the graph is working properly; the column of data can then be deleted before it is finally saved for the children to use.

With the text and numbers in place use the formatting tools to change the font, size, colour and fill colour of the cells. Colour can help with the instructions for the children later on – 'Only type in the purple area'.

The font and fill tools are on the toolbars above in *Excel* and can be accessed via the effects tool **e** on the toolbar in *Softease*.

Select the cell or cells that require formatting before making selections from the toolbar. Cells can be selected by clicking in a single cell, clicking and dragging over several, clicking on the row number or column letter to select a whole row or column, or clicking in the corner square between 1 and A to select the whole sheet. Often cell sizes will alter automatically to accommodate larger writing. If the cell size does need to be changed, the lines between the letters and numbers of the headings can be dragged in *Excel* or anywhere along the line in *Softease*.

How to select data in a spreadsheet and create a graph

Once the table is prepared the graph can be added. First of all select the whole table, including the titles and the data, and then click on the graph wizard tool.

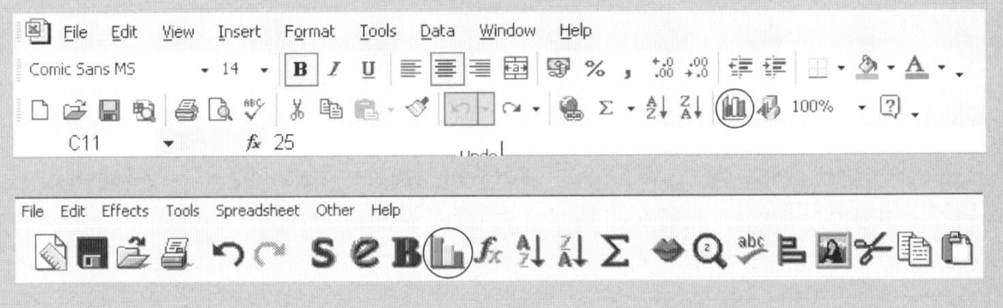

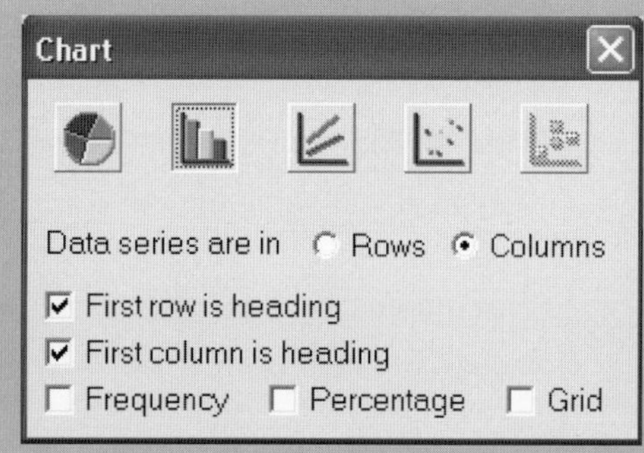

The type of graph can be selected by making choices in the dialogue box which appears. As options are selected the appearance of the graph can be monitored. In *Softease* there are five types of graph which can be chosen by clicking on one of the icons across the top of the **Chart** box. The changes take effect on the graph which appears on the screen as a new object.

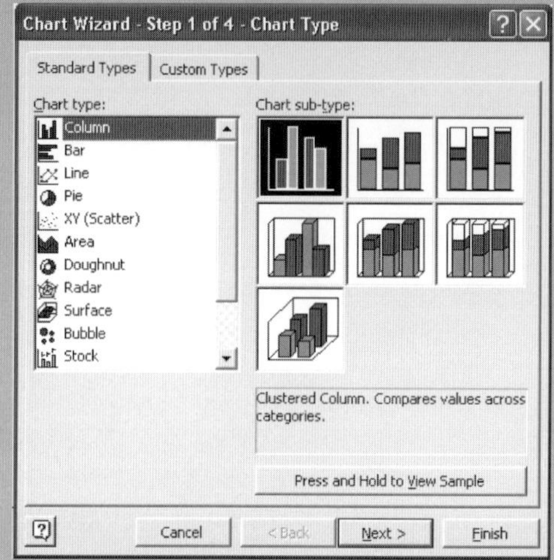

Excel offers a huge range of graphs – called charts – and variations also. As you click **Next** to proceed through the **Chart Wizard** the appearance of the graph is displayed in the dialogue box.

The large number of choices can appear confusing but this is a stage in the process that does not need to be shared with the children and the final spreadsheet is easy to complete.

Both types of spreadsheet software include a legend (or key) by default. In *Softease* the legend is easily removed if it is not required by clicking on it and pressing **Back Space** on the keyboard.

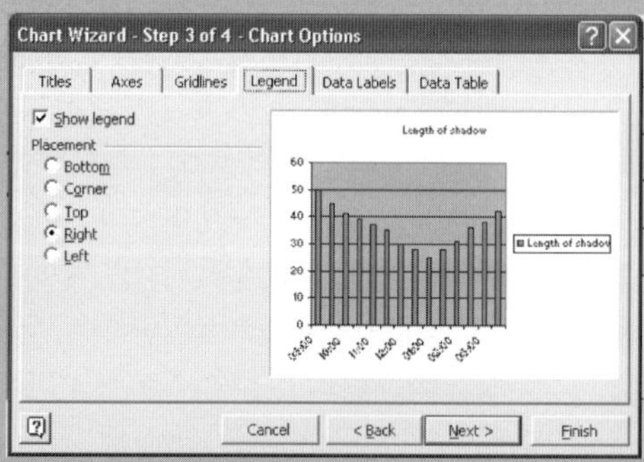

The legend in *Excel* is controlled during the third of the four steps in the **Chart Wizard**. Clicking on the **Legend** tab reveals options which include **Show legend**; by removing the tick, the legend will disappear from the graph. In the final step you need to place the graph as an object in the spreadsheet so that the table and the graph will be visible side by side.

Once choices have been made to ensure that the graph looks as it should, the wizard can be closed.

How to format a graph

Final choices concerning colours of parts of the graph or the font or wording of the labels can be edited if you are using *Excel* by double clicking on the axis, title, bar or element that you wish to change. A format box then appears allowing choices to be made relating to the selected element. In *Softease* the **Effects** tool can be used to open the **Effects** window where you can make changes to selected parts of the graph.

How to lock parts of a spreadsheet

Whether it is planned to use the spreadsheet on a stand-alone computer for groups to use in rotation, to place it on the network for groups to use simultaneously, or as a class activity to be completed collaboratively around the interactive whiteboard, it is a good idea to protect parts of the spreadsheet from being altered by mistake. With the *Softease* spreadsheet the process involves selecting those items that do not want to be changed and selecting **Lock to page** from the **Tools** menu. Include the graph in this process; in that way it cannot be moved although it will change as the results are entered in the correct cells. The only part of the spreadsheet that the children do need to access is the column where the results are to be entered.

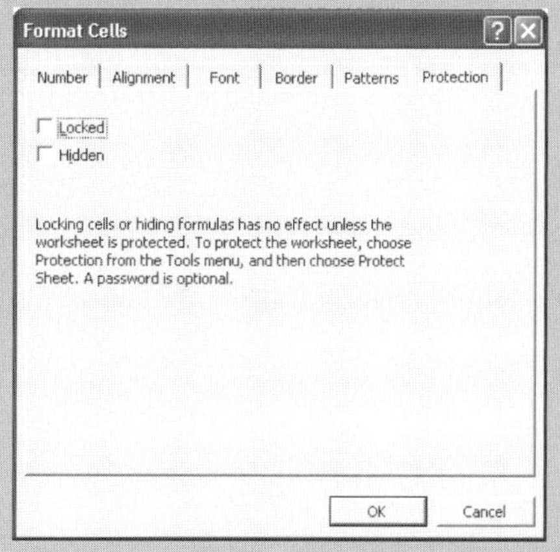

In *Excel* protecting the sheet is a two-part process and it is with the space where the children are to type that you start.

- Select the cells where the results are to be entered and choose **Cells . . .** from the **Format** menu.
- Choose the **Protection** tab in the **Format Cells** dialogue box that appears.
- Make sure that the **Locked** option is not ticked – it is not normally necessary to check all the other cells as the default is locked.
- Click **OK**.

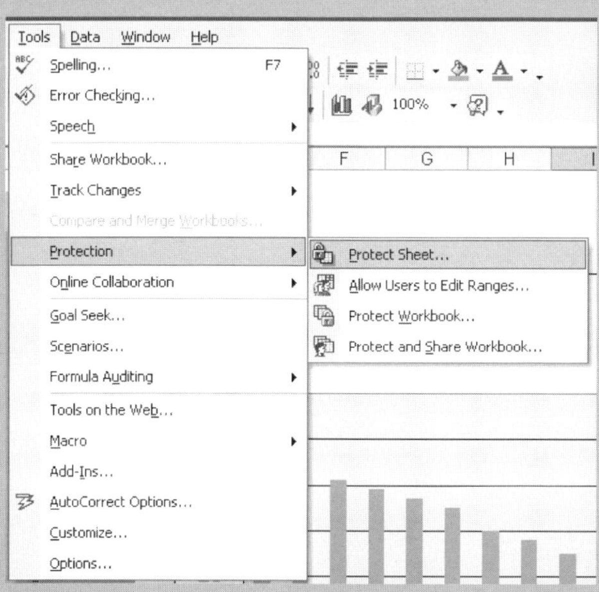

The second step is to protect the spreadsheet by selecting the **Tools** menu and then **Protection** > **Protect Sheet . . .** The level of protection can be chosen and a password if required. With the sheet protected it should be possible to alter the results column but nothing else. Test the sheet by changing some of the results and watching to see that the graph responds. The results can then be deleted, which will cause all the bars to disappear on the graph and then the file can be saved for the final time.

How to make a 'Read-only' file

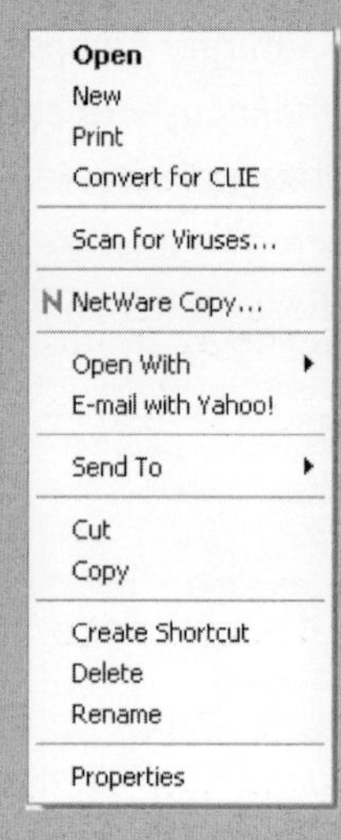

Another way to ensure that a file that you have created for the children to use is not altered or accidentally deleted is to make it a 'Read-only' file once you have completed it and saved it. The children will be able to open the file and work with it in the normal way, but clicking **Save** will prompt the children to give the file a new name and open the **Save As . . .** dialogue box. In that way the next group will always find the file ready as you made it.

The file needs to be closed before you start this operation. Open the folder that the file is stored in and right click on the file icon. A menu should appear which includes the option **Properties** at the bottom.

Select **Properties** and in the **Attributes** section tick the **Read-only** box and then click **OK**. The file is now Read-only.

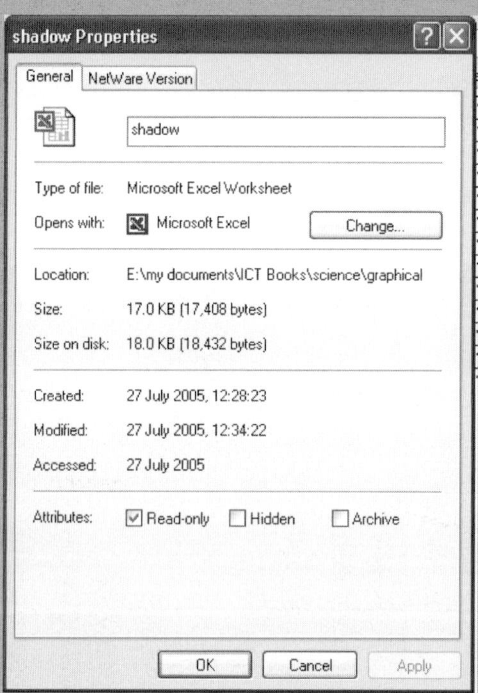

How to transfer a graph to a word processor

If it is decided that the children's investigation is to be recorded and shared using ICT, then the graphs that they have drawn can easily be incorporated in most word processors by selecting the graph, copying it and then selecting **Paste** in the word processor.

What will the children learn?

To use ICT to enter data in a spreadsheet and present findings

One of the ultimate goals in the development of ICT capability is that children will select software to help them undertake tasks and solve problems. Activities of this kind help them to see the potential benefits of a spreadsheet in a supported way.

That data represented graphically can be easier to understand than textual data

Careful selection of data and graph types can help to make patterns in children's results very visual. Draw children's attention to the fact that patterns which were not obvious in the table became clear when the graph was drawn.

That information represented as graphs can be interpreted and analysed to provide answers to questions

Too often graphs are seen as an end point rather than a means to an end. Making sure that children voice their ideas and predictions at the start of an investigation will help them to use the graphical information to provide answers.

That information comes from a variety of sources and can be presented in a variety of forms

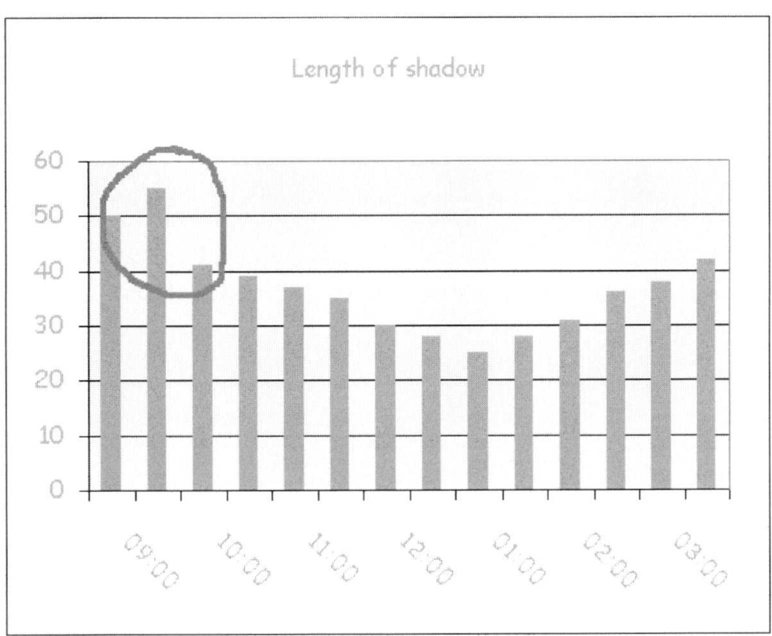

Inaccurate data stands out in the graph

One of the key reasons for using ICT in this context is that it enables children to remain focused on the source of the information and not get lost in the process of creating a graph. By using a bar chart to represent shadows, the connection between the initial measurement and the form of presentation can be emphasised.

To identify and correct implausible and inaccurate data

By creating graphs, data which do not fit a pattern can be easily identified. Consider making mistakes in recording numbers to help the children spot anomalies.

That ICT can be used for collecting, storing and sorting information in an organised way

Aim to make sure that there is a reason to return to the stored data to stress how useful it is to keep it in this format. There are many other tools in a spreadsheet which can help to put a collection of numbers in rank order. Look for other connections by sorting data into subsets.

Challenging the more able and supporting the less able: modifying the project for older and younger pupils

By supporting children with this task all should be able to turn their measurements into a graph and talk about what it means. Try to make sure that children do not avoid the ICT task altogether; use it as a tool to help their understanding, not as an additional complexity. Reading results to children so that they can focus on entering them and watching the graph grow will help. If you conduct a discussion of the way that the spreadsheet was prepared, either with the whole class, or informally, it will support children as they learn to describe their ICT use. Aim to sow seeds for the future by drawing the children's attention to the graph-making function of the spreadsheet and how else it could be used. Some children need time to understand the logic behind tables. Explain the layout of the table carefully and remind them of any recent experiences of tally charts or timetables. Explaining and analysing what the graph means, making the connection with the numbers and the measurements that the numbers represent, will need to be modelled time and again for some children.

Children who are curious and capable of being more independent in their use of ICT should be encouraged to take over elements of the creation of the spreadsheet. By exploring alternatives and selecting the type of graph that will best display the data, they will begin to learn how to use the spreadsheet independently. Make sure that opportunities to save and amend the data are exploited appropriately for the ICT level that children are working at; encouraging children to compare the spreadsheet task with their own graph drawing, for example, will provide Level 4 assessment opportunities.

Why teach this?

ICT makes an important contribution to scientific research at all levels and this type of information-handling task is an ICT opportunity that is accessible to children at Key Stage 2. The focus of this activity is section 1 of the ICT NC KS2

PoS, 'Finding things out'. The children gather their own information, and use ICT to store, process and retrieve it. There are also opportunities to address section 3, 'Exchanging and sharing information', if they continue to use ICT to present the findings of their investigations.

Although the QCA scheme of work introduces spreadsheets at Year 5 (5D: *Introduction to spreadsheets*), by working with a ready-prepared spreadsheet this activity scaffolds the use of ICT as a way of assisting with the presentation of data, so that the children can focus on the interpretation of their results. The activity builds on the content of QCA ICT Scheme of Work Units 1E: *Representing information graphically: pictograms*, and 2E: *Questions and answers*. It develops similar ICT skills as Units 3A: *Combining text and graphics* and 4D: *Collecting and presenting information: questionnaires and pie charts*. It also provides a useful link to Units 5B: *Analysing data and asking questions: using complex searches* and 5C: *Evaluating information, checking accuracy and questioning plausibility*.

The project supports Science NC KS2 PoS Sc1, particularly the investigative skills 2f–l. By supporting the handling of experimental data it will also contribute to scientific understanding by allowing the children to focus on using their scientific knowledge to explain what their findings mean. The task can be adapted to apply to any investigation where numerical data are collected in the QCA scheme of work units for science.

See also *Maths* Project 2 (*Counting*), *Maths* Project 6 (*Statistical investigations 1*) and *Maths* Project 9 (*Patterns and spreadsheets*).

Project Fact Card: Project 6: Giant's hand

Who is it for?

- 8- to 11-year-olds (NC Levels 2–4)

What will the children do?

- Presented with an enlarged handprint in the context of a story, the children are invited to predict some of the other personal measurements of the person who made it. They are then required to design and carry out an investigation that would support their predictions using graphs of other children's measurements

What should the children know already?

- How to enter data
- That ICT can help to draw graphs

What do I need to know?

- How to set up and format a table in a spreadsheet
- How to create and format a scatter graph using a spreadsheet
- How to add a trend line to a scatter graph
- How to discuss implausible data with children

What resources will I need?

- Spreadsheet software such as *Microsoft Excel* or BlackCat *NumberBox 2*

What will the children learn?

- That data represented graphically can be easier to understand than textual data
- To use ICT to classify information and present findings
- To use straightforward lines of enquiry
- That information can be represented as graphs but that this can only provide limited answers to questions
- That collecting and storing information in an organised way helps them find answers to questions and present findings
- To work with others to interpret information
- That lines of best fit can suggest patterns and relationships between measurements
- To interpret and analyse information in graphs
- To use ICT to test a hypothesis and to identify and correct implausible and inaccurate data

How to challenge the more able

- Require a wider range of evidence to support their predictions
- Design their own enquiry and spreadsheet to display results

How to support the less able

- Provide spreadsheet templates for children to enter data
- Reduce the number of measurements

Why teach this?

- The project aims to use ICT to identify, prepare and interpret information as described in ICT NC KS2 PoS statements 1a–c. It also highlights the necessity for *Reviewing, modifying and evaluating work as it progresses* identified in section 4.
- The project builds on the content of QCA ICT Scheme of Work Unit 4D and addresses elements of Units 5A, 5B, 5C and 5D.
- Although working with fictional evidence, this project involves plenty of real scientific enquiry. It focuses on Science NC KS' PoS statements for Sc1: using observations and measurements (1b) and the planning and interpretive skills (2a, 2b, 2g–j). The use of ICT to present evidence and support predictions is required by the Science National Curriculum. With a focus on Sc1 in a fictional context, the investigative skills developed can be applied to a number of contexts in the QCA scheme of work or the concept of 'forensic scientist' adapted to match other science content.

PROJECT 6

Giant's hand

What will the children do?

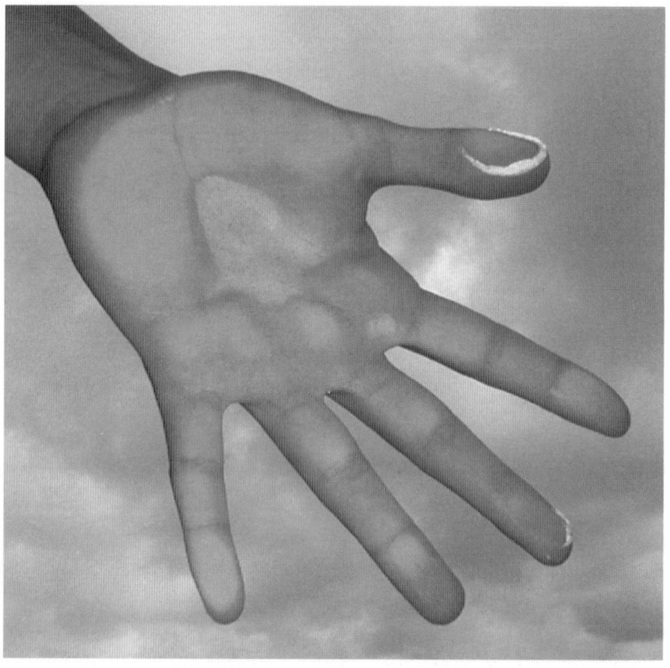

You can also reduce a hand-print to suggest that fairies have been at school!

There are a number of ways that evidence of a 'giant' can be presented to the children. One scenario is that a huge handprint has been captured on the school photocopier and that the class as expert forensic scientists have been asked to provide a description of the person who left it. The 'evidence' is created by enlisting the enlarge facility on the photocopier to provide each group with a copy of the print.

The initial discussions need to explore possible ways that the enquiry may proceed. These can be undertaken as a class exercise, or, alternatively, an element of competition or rivalry between the groups can be introduced. If the children have had no experience of spreadsheets before, then an example chart showing how two sets of personal measurements can be compared could be demonstrated. As the focus of this activity is on interpreting results and supporting predictions it is possible for valuable learning to accrue even if the children are using ready-prepared spreadsheets and only entering their own measurements and interpreting the graphs that are produced. The appropriate level of challenge is achieved for groups and individuals by handing over some or all of the creation of the spreadsheet. The complexity of the task set can also be adjusted by setting specific questions – 'How big would the giant's shoes/hat/chair be?' – or more open-ended investigations – 'What can we say about the owner of this hand?' – leaving the children to decide which measurements they are going to take.

Activity 1: Preparing the spreadsheet

Once the children have planned their investigation and taken personal measurements, the spreadsheet that they are going to use needs to be adapted or created, to accommodate the data that they have collected. If the children have been provided with a template including a graph, then the graph will be drawn automatically as they enter the data. If the creation of the graph is part of the children's learning, then time will need to be allowed for them to do so.

Activity 2: Interpreting the data

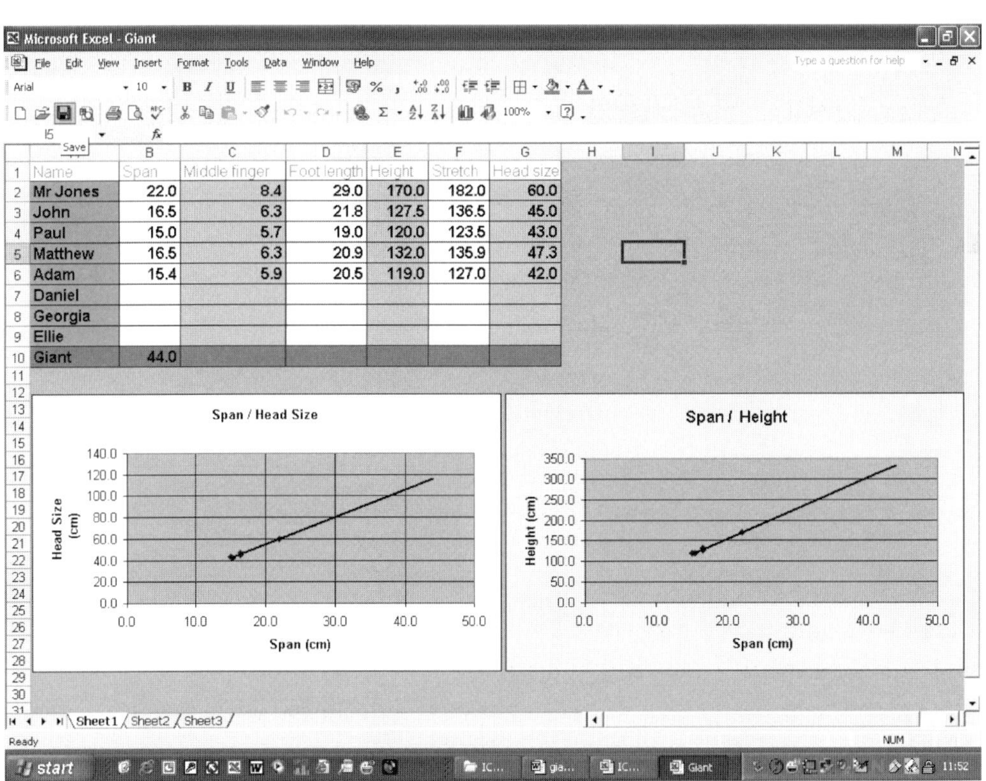

Microsoft Excel - Giant
File Edit View Insert Format Tools Data Window Help
Name | Span | Middle finger | Foot length | Height | Stretch | Head size
Mr Jones | 22.0 | 8.4 | 29.0 | 170.0 | 182.0 | 60.0
John | 16.5 | 6.3 | 21.8 | 127.5 | 136.5 | 45.0
Paul | 15.0 | 5.7 | 19.0 | 120.0 | 123.5 | 43.0
Matthew | 16.5 | 6.3 | 20.9 | 132.0 | 135.9 | 47.3
Adam | 15.4 | 5.9 | 20.5 | 119.0 | 127.0 | 42.0
Daniel
Georgia
Ellie
Giant | 44.0
Span / Head Size
Head Size (cm)
Span (cm)
Span / Height
Height (cm)
Span (cm)
Sheet1 Sheet2 Sheet3
Ready
NUM
start
11:52

The second activity – and arguably the most important – is the interpretation of the graphs.

You may prefer to do this with paper copies so that the children can extend lines of best fit and make predictions by drawing with pencils and rulers on the printout.

Further use of ICT could be added to the activity by requiring the children to construct a report or presentation of their findings with the graphs inserted.

What should the children know already?

How to enter data

The simplest level of ICT use in this project involves children entering data to an existing table. Recognising that the keys pressed on the keyboard will be inserted in the active cell and that a cell is selected by clicking on it will help them add data independently.

That ICT can help to draw graphs

Children should be familiar with ICT-generated graphs from work with simple bar charts in Key Stage 1. It may be necessary to plot some data manually to reassure the children that the computer can represent their data accurately.

An example spreadsheet is available on the CD-ROM accompanying this book. A 'Handling Data' booklet is also available (see Project 5 on the CD-ROM).

What do I need to know?

How to set up and format a table in a spreadsheet

While spreadsheets are designed to work with columns and rows of numbers and it takes very little time to create row and column headings, it is worth while spending some time formatting the cell colour and font to help young children with entering data. The process described here uses *Microsoft Excel* but most spreadsheets have similar functions. For details on formatting cells in *Excel* and *Softease Spreadsheet*, see *What do I need to know?* in Project 5.

How to create and format a scatter graph using a spreadsheet

With the data entered in the table the two measurements that you want to compare must be selected before the graph is created.

	A	B	C	D	E	F	G
1	Name	Span	Middle finger	Foot length	Height	Stretch	Head size
2	Mr Jones	22.0	8.4	29.0	170.0	182.0	60.0
3	John	16.5	6.3	21.8	127.5	136.5	45.0
4	Paul	15.0	5.7	19.0	120.0	123.5	43.0
5	Matthew	16.1	6.3	20.9	132.0	135.9	47.3
6	Adam	15.4	5.9	20.5	119.0	127.0	42.0
7	Daniel						
8	Georgia						
9	Ellie						
10	Giant	44.0					

Adjacent columns can be selected by clicking and dragging to highlight them. If the columns do not lie side by side, then they can be selected by dragging over the first column and then holding down **Ctrl** on the keyboard while the second column is selected. If you select the headings too, these will be added to the graph. To create the graph, click on the Chart Wizard tool and a series of dialogue boxes will allow you to make choices about the type and layout of your graph.

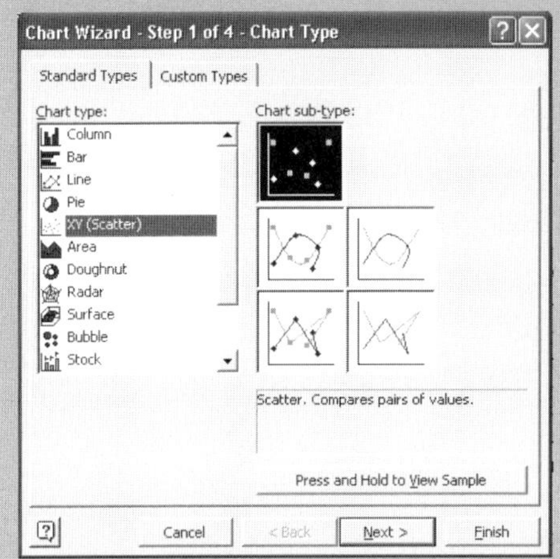

First of all choose the type of graph that you require. The XY scatter graph will plot pairs of numbers revealing whether there is a relationship between the two measurements. Positive correlations will appear clustered around a line sloping upwards to the right – as one measurement increases so does the other. Most body measurements which grow in proportion will display this type of relationship.

Clicking **Next** in the Chart Wizard will enable changes to be made to the data selected.

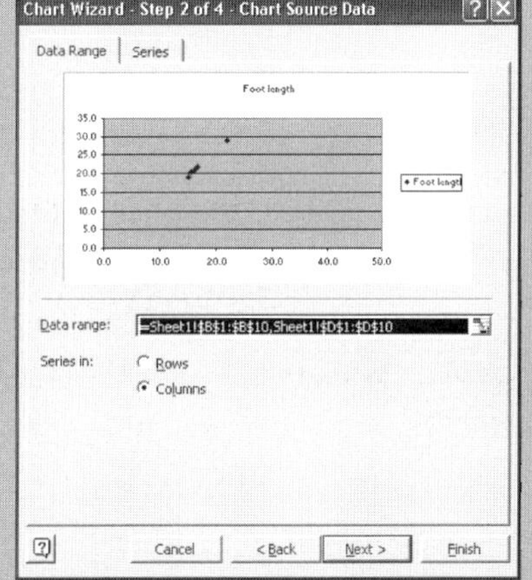

If the graph is to compare data in two rows rather than two columns then changing the series will be reflected in the miniature version of the graph in the wizard.

Clicking **Next** takes you to the third step of the wizard where axis titles and other choices can be made. Elements of the finished chart can be altered by right clicking on the part that you wish to change, so do not worry if you forget to do something.

The titles of the chart and axes are entered in the appropriate boxes and the gridlines that you want displayed can be selected here. The **Legend** tab allows you to remove the legend or position it. Each change that you make should be reflected in the miniature version, so keep checking to see that the graph appears as it should. Once the basic layout is completed to your satisfaction **Next** takes you to the final stage where you can decide whether you want the graph to appear alongside the data as an object on the spreadsheet or whether you want it to be placed as a new sheet which you would access by clicking on a tab at the bottom of the page.

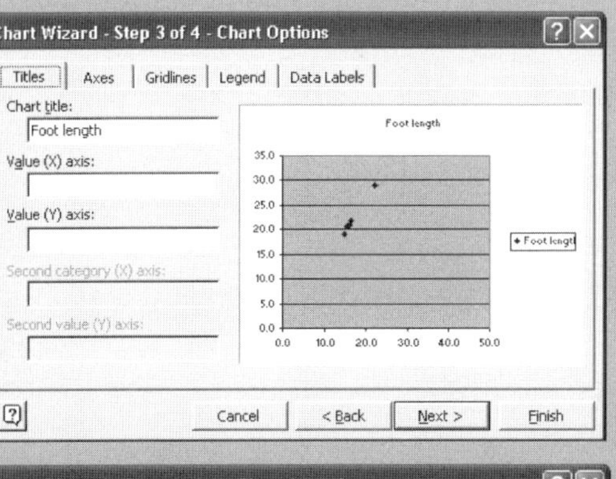

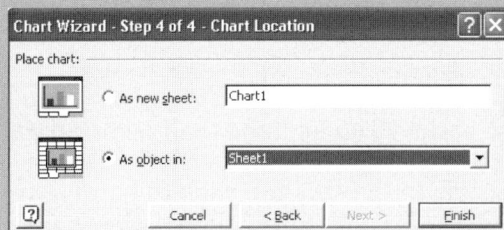

Where the graph is going to be used by children adding data and watching the graph grow, it is best for the graph to be an object on the sheet. Clicking **Finish** will close the wizard and complete the graph. Changes can be made to backgrounds, titles and axes by right clicking on the part you wish to amend and selecting **Format**.

How to add a trend line to a scatter graph

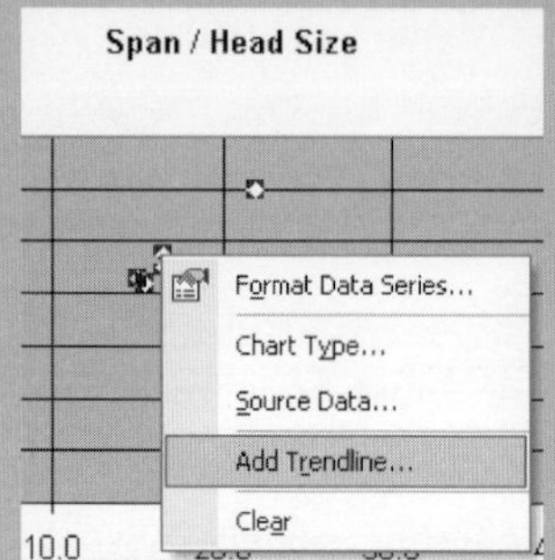

Right clicking on one of the plotted co-ordinates on a scatter graph will produce a short menu with an option to **Add Trendline . . .** The trend line or line of best fit tries to make sense of the data and indicate any relationship. It may be better for children to add this to a printout by hand when they are trying to extrapolate from their data what size the giant may have been.

How to discuss implausible data with children

One of the important parts of this activity is questioning and making sense of data. Children are often less likely to accept that a mistake has been made on a professional-looking graph. The recognition that the computer does what it is told and does not 'think' is a key lesson. Data can be checked as they are entered but often wild inaccuracies caused by measuring from the wrong end of a metre stick or reading the wrong scale, for example, can slip through to the graph where they should make the children raise questions.

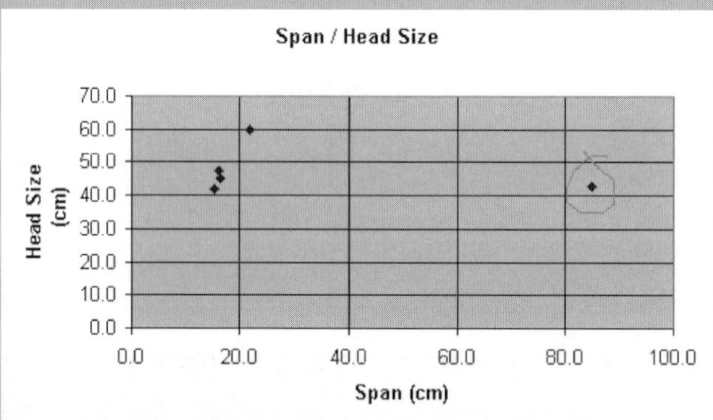

One of the real values of ICT in this type of activity is the way that plotting and drawing are supported by the technology to enable the children's full attention to focus on the interpretation and analysis of the data.

What will the children learn?

That data represented graphically can be easier to understand than textual data

Trends and patterns not immediately visible in the children's tables become very visible in scatter graphs.

To use ICT to classify information and present findings

The problem-based approach to this task makes the use of ICT to produce graphs a step along the way to presenting their justification for their prediction. The lesson that organising their measurements in such a way that ICT can help them to present findings is a valuable one for young scientists to learn.

To use straightforward lines of enquiry

The initial discussions that explore the way that the children are going to proceed with collecting and presenting their evidence are very important. Open questions and testing of the reliability of suggestions are also important – aim to show that several measurements will make the prediction more reliable.

That information can be represented as graphs but that this can only provide limited answers to questions

The interpretation of the graphical information is necessary in this activity as no proof is achieved, only a theory.

That collecting and storing information in an organised way helps them find answers to questions and present findings

The organisation demanded by the software provides valuable learning for future investigations with or without ICT.

To work with others to interpret information

The interpretation of their findings should be a collaborative and possibly noisy affair. Persuade children to articulate what the graphs mean to them and to listen to the views of others.

That lines of best fit can suggest patterns and relationships between measurements

Aim to use examples of personal measurements from individuals to indicate patterns in the data.

To interpret and analyse information in graphs

The information that a graph contains is key to this project. Some explanation of the graphs that they have produced will be necessary to support their predictions.

To use ICT to test a hypothesis and to identify and correct implausible and inaccurate data

The prediction that there is a relationship between some element of hand measurement and other body measurements will need to be justified if the group are to go on to make an estimate of other dimensions of the 'giant'. Inaccuracies cannot be guaranteed but can be 'arranged' to ensure children learn to spot errors.

Challenging the more able and supporting the less able: modifying the project for older and younger pupils

It is possible to make this type of investigation suitably challenging for Year 6 children and, through the provision of prepared spreadsheet templates, for children to enter the measurements that they make, simple enough for Year 4 children to produce graphs. The harder part of the task is the interpretation and justification of the claim that they may make for the size of the 'giant'. Data-handling exercises of this sort need to reflect the cyclical nature of the data-handling process to integrate the stages of the enquiry and maintain a focus on the purpose of processing the data. Reducing the number of measurements through focusing on one relationship can help to support younger children.

Older children can be expected to build a fuller picture of the appearance of the giant based on their measurements of the hand. Also, where the sample of measurements that they have taken does not provide conclusive evidence of a connection, a wider range of evidence to support their predictions can be demanded.

The more involvement the children have in the design of their own enquiry and spreadsheet to display results, the greater the benefit to learning and assessment in both science and ICT. Some may also decide on the type of graph that they are going to use and be expected to justify their sample size. Turning the classroom into a courtroom where our forensic scientists have to justify their findings and present them in role can be an additional challenge for others.

Why teach this?

This is a fun project which provides a child-oriented context in which to use ICT to identify, prepare and interpret information as described in ICT NC KS2 PoS statements 1a–c. It helps the children make sense of the need for *Reviewing, modifying and evaluating work as it progresses* identified in section 4 of the National Curriculum. The opportunities to compare their use of ICT with other methods of creating graphs are extensive, as are reflections on the use of ICT in society.

The project builds on the content of QCA ICT Scheme of Work Unit 4D: *Collecting and presenting information: questionnaires and pie charts* and addresses elements of Units 5A: *Graphical modelling*, 5B: *Analysing data and asking questions: using complex searches*, 5C: *Evaluating information, checking accuracy and questioning plausibility* and 5D: *Introduction to spreadsheets.*

Although the children are working with fictional evidence, this project involves plenty of real scientific enquiry and practical measurement. It focuses on Science NC KS2 PoS statements for Sc1: using observations and measurements (1b) and the planning and interpretive skills (2a, 2b, 2g–m). The evaluation of the enquiries can be used to address Sc1, 2m in particular and provides good opportunities for the assessment of Sc1 to Level 4. The spreadsheet is an appropriate use of ICT to present evidence and support predictions as required by the science National Curriculum. With a focus on Sc1 in a fictional context, the investigative skills developed can be applied to a number of contexts in the QCA scheme of work or the concept of 'forensic scientist' adapted to match other science content, for example trying to identify the possible origin of a dandelion leaf based on a survey of the school field.

See also *Maths* Project 9 (*Patterns and spreadsheets*) and *Maths* Project 10 (*Statistical investigations 2*) for related activities.

Project Fact Card: Project 7: Multimedia information source

Who is it for?

- 7- to 9-year-olds (NC Levels 2–4)

What will the children do?

- In groups the children will create their own section of a computer-based information source using *PowerPoint*. The individual sections can be then linked to create a class resource. The project will involve research into a science topic and the collecting and processing of a variety of media including textual, graphical, sound and video information

What should the children know already?

- Familiarity with navigating through CD-ROM encyclopaedias
- How to save and retrieve files
- How to make selections through menus and icons
- How to select, move and resize objects

What do I need to know?

- How to plan and structure a multimedia resource
- How to design a slide layout in *PowerPoint*
- How to insert text, images, video and sound into *PowerPoint* presentations
- How to create links between slides using action buttons
- How to ensure that only action buttons advance slides
- How to make links between *PowerPoint* presentations

What resources will I need?

- *PowerPoint* or similar presentation software
- Microphones
- Digital still and video cameras

What will the children learn?

- That information comes from a variety of sources and can be presented in a variety of forms
- That sounds convey information and that pictures provide information
- That computers use icons to provide information and instructions
- To use ICT appropriately to communicate ideas through text
- To select and use different techniques to communicate ideas through pictures
- That ICT can be used to capture and present sounds
- To use ICT to organise, reorganise and analyse ideas and information
- That a screen image can be a finished product
- To select suitable information and media and prepare it for processing using ICT
- To use a multimedia authoring program to organise, refine and present information in different forms for a specific audience

How to challenge the more able

- Involve able children in the structuring and creation of the class resource which connects all the groups' work
- Help them to create original sound and movie files

How to support the less able

- Provide a presentation template differentiating the tasks left to complete

Why teach this?

- The project covers the breadth of the ICT NC KS2 PoS very well. Elements of statements 1a–c, 2a and 3a, 3b can all be addressed and the opportunity to discuss the strengths and weaknesses of the use of ICT for creating this type of information source can make a valuable contribution to the 'Reviewing, modifying and evaluating work as it progresses' strand of the ICT PoS.
- The content of QCA ICT Scheme of Work Units 3A, 3B and 4A can be extended and combined for a real purpose through this project.
- The project makes a novel use of presentation software to support teaching and learning of almost any science topic. The children's level of science understanding can be developed and assessed through the process of representing their scientific knowledge using ICT. An information source of this type will enhance any of the QCA scheme of work units.

PROJECT 7

Multimedia information source

What will the children do?

Increasingly as 'internaughts' – users of the internet – children are consumers and readers of hyperlinked multimedia information. This project helps them to become authors in that genre and provides a meaningful and fun context for them to acquire and display their scientific knowledge and understanding. With help and guidance, all stages of the process are accessible to Key Stage 2 children; however, to provide support or manage time the initial planning and structure may be prepared beforehand.

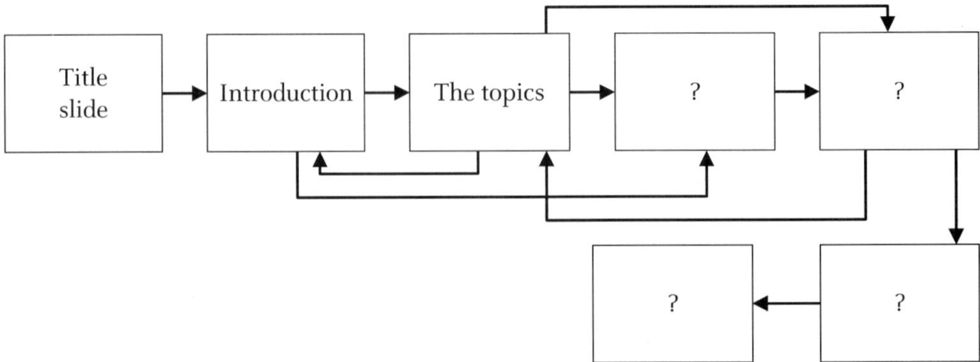

PowerPoint was originally designed as presentation software to create slides for projection. The ability to switch off the automatic progression when clicking anywhere on the slide and place buttons on the screen which can be instructed to link to specific slides or other presentations makes it a versatile piece of software. If information is not going to be presented in a linear format – page 1, page 2, page 3, etc. – then some initial planning such as the diagram above is required. The visual interface that *PowerPoint* provides can be very helpful with this planning as its key educational use in this instance is as a thought processor, helping the children to make connections using their understanding of the topic. So, although an initial plan helps, the provisional nature of ICT makes it easy to reorder information at a later stage and create or remove links.

Time constraints make it difficult for children to produce a complete resource on any science topic, but by dividing the task into sections of a class resource, each group has a more manageable workload and the necessary collaboration enhances the activity. The content of the task could be explaining the results of an investigation – for example, where each group had grown plants under different conditions – or from research using books and other secondary sources to create a resource about the solar system where each group researches a planet, for example.

Activity 1: First gather your ingredients

Once the initial class discussion about the overall structure of the resource has been completed the groups can undertake paper-based planning for their section. The first ICT activity is then to search for and assemble the different media that they are going to use through internet searches, reading, taking digital pictures, recording video or sounds, depending on the topic. Careful management of files can be helped by creating folders for each group and stressing the importance of naming files so that they can be easily located.

Activity 2: Assemble the information

With the resources saved the groups can then begin to create their part of the resource. Some groups may start with a blank *PowerPoint* file; others may be given a template to start with. A presentation containing the number of slides required needs to be created and each slide given a title.

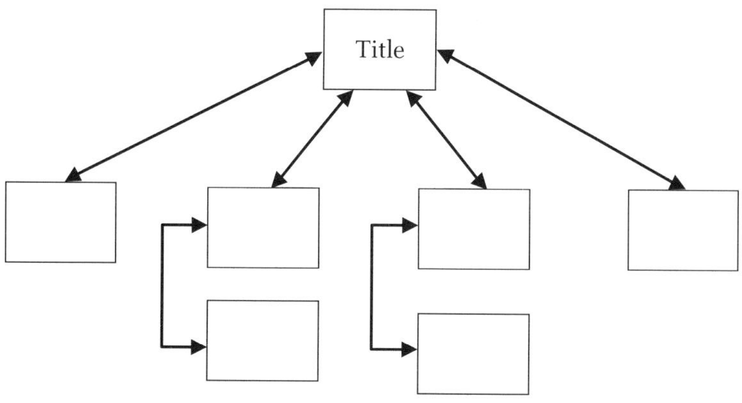

The pictures and resources can then be added to the appropriate slides and text inserted in text boxes.

Activity 3: Creating links

Using action buttons the links between the relevant slides are added, remembering to include links back so that readers can navigate through the information. The final linking together of all the groups' sections can be undertaken by one of the groups or the teacher once all sections are completed and saved. It is important for children to use the resource once it is completed so that evaluation and discussion of the effects of their choices can be undertaken.

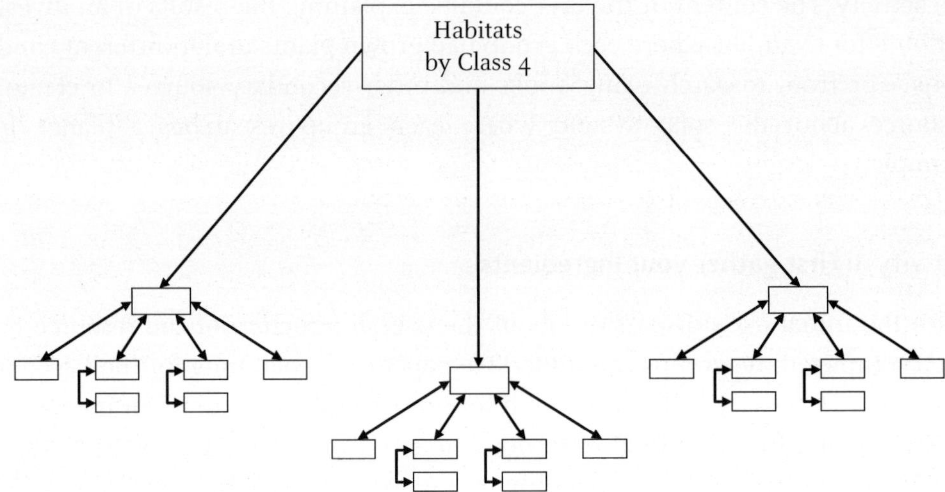

What should the children know already?

Familiarity with navigating through CD-ROM encyclopaedias

An understanding of the way that information can be linked can be gained from using any computer-based information source. Discuss with the children the way they know which buttons to press and point out the convention of underlining links on web pages.

How to save and retrieve files

Even simple projects can use a number of different images and other resource files. Drawing on children's previous experience of saving their work will help them to learn about different file types and how to use **Save As . . .** to place a file in a particular directory or folder.

How to make selections through menus and icons

Children should be becoming familiar with windows environments now and recognise the need to select tools or give commands by clicking on the toolbars and using the menus. Through this project they will also learn how to create icons that 'work'.

How to select, move and resize objects

Previous work that the children have carried out with drawing software or desktop publishers will help them to ensure that the screens that they create are laid out clearly, as changes can be made to the position and size of an object.

What do I need to know?

How to plan and structure a multimedia resource

With non-linear information there is a discipline required in designing the structure and writing the text. If there is more than one route to information, then the sequence in which information is encountered may be different for different readers. The testing of the resource to ensure that the information makes sense is a valuable experience for the children. The project also needs to be kept to a reasonable size for the time available. Three pages interlinked involve the creation of six action buttons. With younger children it is possible to create a framework file with links already in place for them to add text and images; but it is important to ensure that the ICT requirements of the project are sufficiently challenging, so beware of preparing too much. Class projects can soon grow in terms of the memory that they require to save them, especially if video clips are involved. Plan ahead to ensure that all the resources can be saved to the same server or hard drive; a large USB pen drive or CD-ROM may be needed to transport the finished files.

How to design a slide layout in *PowerPoint*

If you have never used *PowerPoint* before, do not worry – it is relatively easy! Starting the software will present you with the option to create a new file either using a ready-made template or blank and will then present you with a range of formats for your first slide; selecting one and clicking **OK** will open the software in 'Normal view' where you can see your first slide and edit it. There are three key views in *PowerPoint* which can either be selected from the **View** menu or by using the icons in the bottom left-hand corner of the screen. From left to right, these are:

- Normal
- Slide Sorter – which shows all the slides in miniature, allowing you to drag them to reposition them
- Slide Show – which runs the presentation and enables the buttons and effects to be tested

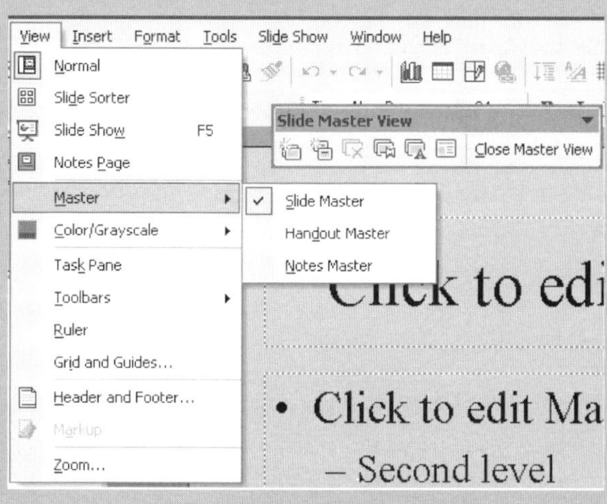

There is another view accessible from the **View** menu which allows you to access the **Slide Master**. The **Master** controls the background and style of all slides. If you wanted a button or image to appear on all slides, then inserting it on the **Master** not only inserts it on all existing slides, but also on any new ones which are subsequently created. Once any changes to the **Master** have been completed click **Close Master View** and insert the required number of slides by selecting **New Slide** from the **Insert** menu or the **New Slide** icon on the right of the screen. Choose a suitable layout for the information; it is best to use a layout with at least a title text box because whatever is typed in the title box will become the name of the slide, which is useful when creating links later on.

How to insert text, images, video and sound into *PowerPoint* presentations

The range of media that you prepare and incorporate in the resource is one of the ways of differentiating the complexity of the task. When in the **Normal** view information in a variety of forms can be added by selecting the type of information from the **Insert** menu.

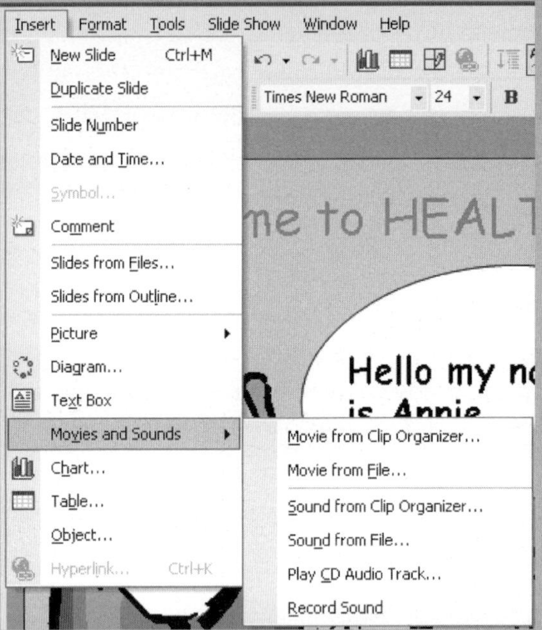

Text

Select **Text Box** and then click and drag the box of the required size and shape on the slide. Type in the text; text boxes, like all objects, can be resized by clicking and dragging the handles, or moved by dragging on the grey border.

Images

Select **Picture** > **From File ...** and navigate to locate the image file that you require. Collecting your resources in one folder, like good cooks assemble their ingredients before they start, makes this task far easier as the software will automatically take you to the last folder accessed. After you have located your resource folder for the first time, subsequent resources are easily inserted. The software supports a range of picture formats, and images can come from digital photographs, paint or drawing files, scanned images or files downloaded from the internet.

> Images located on a web page can often be saved to your computer by right clicking with the mouse on the picture that you require. **Select Save Picture As ...** from the menu that appears and save to your resource folder.

Video

Select **Movies and Sounds** > **Movie from File** . . . Select the movie file and click **OK** – it is possible for the video to play as soon as the slide opens or when you click on it. Videos can also be downloaded from the internet or be produced by the children (see Projects 2 and 8).

Sound

Sounds can be added to the resource in a number of ways. Selecting **Movies and Sounds** > **Sound from File** . . . from the **Insert** menu will allow you to select a sound file that you have previously saved and choose for it to play as the slide opens or when the icon that appears on the slide is clicked. If the computer has a microphone attached, it is also possible to record sounds by selecting **Record Sound** from the Insert menu.

Another way to play sounds in the resource is to assign the sound to a picture that you have inserted on the slide. Right click on the image on the screen and a menu will appear.

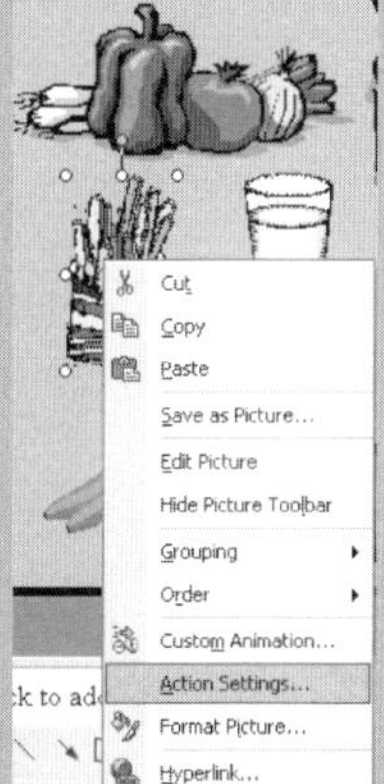

Selecting **Action Settings** . . . displays a dialogue box that enables sounds to be selected that will play each time the picture is clicked. If you wish to play a sound file that you have previously saved then choose **Other Sound** . . . from the drop-down option under **Play sound:** and you can navigate to the file that you require. This method will only play files in the WAV format while the **Insert** menu method supports other formats as well.

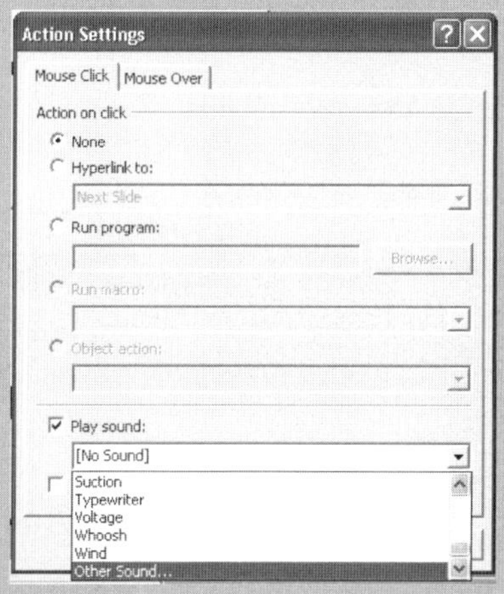

How to create links between slides using action buttons

In **Presentation View** *PowerPoint* normally proceeds through the slides in a presentation in order each time you click on a slide. For this type of resource, however, we want the reader to be able to choose which slide to proceed to and also provide the alternative for them to go back. Links can be created in a number of ways, one of which is to place 'action buttons' on the slide. To add an action button select **Action Buttons** from the **Slide Show** menu and choose the design that you need; choosing the blank **Custom** button shape will allow text to be added to the button later.

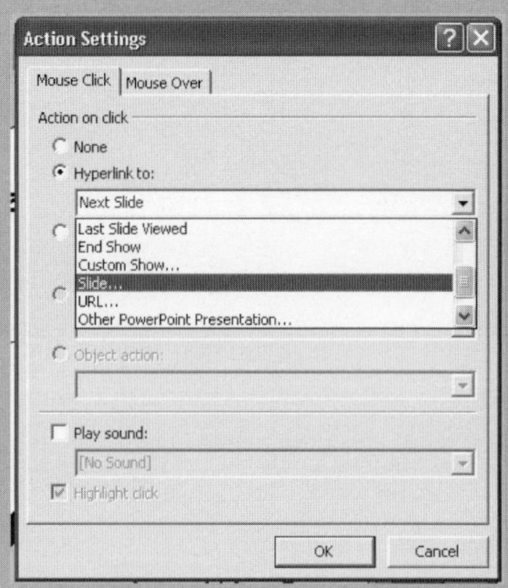

A button of the desired size can then be drawn on the slide by clicking and dragging. As soon as the button is drawn the **Action Settings** dialogue box will appear.

By selecting **Hyperlink to:** a range of options becomes available via the drop-down menu. For this type of resource you need to select **Slide . . .** in order to choose the slide that the button is to open. If titles have been added to the slides, then they will appear in the list; if not – as in the example below – the available slides will be numbered. Clicking on a slide in the list, however, displays a miniature version so that even without titles you can check that the correct slide has been selected before clicking **OK**.

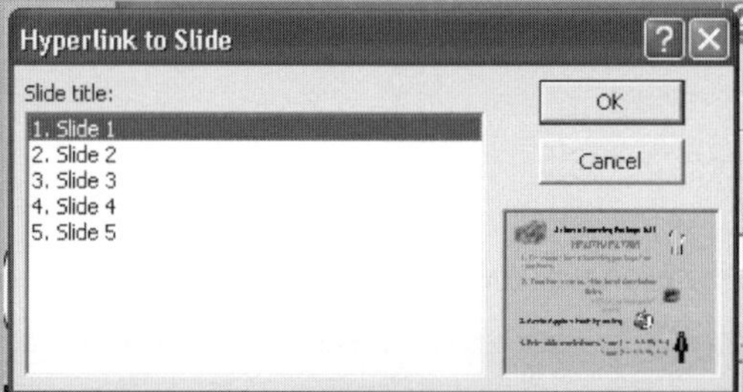

In order to test the action button the presentation must be run by selecting **Presentation View.** In order to return to **Normal View** to add the rest of the buttons, press Escape (Esc) on the keyboard or right click and select **End Show**, or click on the icon that appears in the bottom left-hand corner of the screen and choose **End Show** from there.

Place and check the other action buttons in the same way to enable navigation through the information in the slide show.

How to ensure that only action buttons advance slides

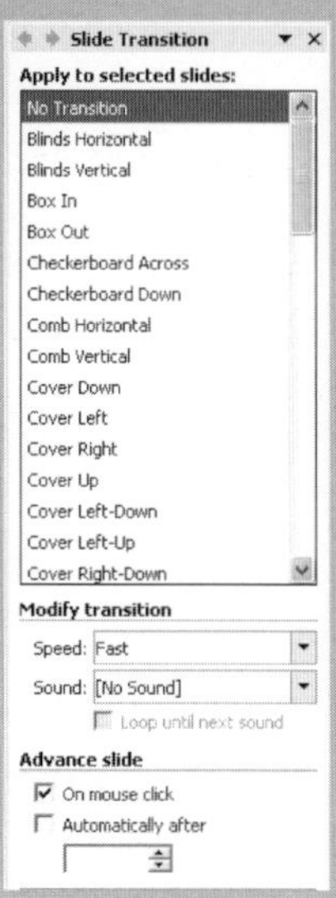

Even with the action buttons in place, clicking somewhere else on the slide will cause the presentation to advance to the next slide. To avoid accidental clicks on the screen displaying a new slide, the slide transition needs to be altered. From the **Slide Show** menu select **Side Transition . . .** and a pane like the one on the right will appear. Removing the tick beside 'On mouse click' stops the current slide from advancing; if 'Apply to All Slides' at the bottom of the pane is clicked only the action buttons in the presentation will make new slides appear.

How to make links between *PowerPoint* presentations

To make the class project work smoothly it helps for each group to produce its own self-contained section of the resource as a separate *PowerPoint* file. Another *PowerPoint* file can then be created as a type of menu or contents page to link to each of the groups' presentations.

Once the menu has been created as a separate *PowerPoint* file it needs to be saved in the same folder as the children's work and all the files will need to be moved together if the links between the files are to work. The process of linking to each group's information is almost the same as the creation of the action buttons described above, except in this instance instead of **Hyperlink to: > Slide . . .** you choose **Hyperlink to: > Other PowerPoint Presentation . . .** Browse to locate the *PowerPoint* that you want to link to and click **OK**. The list of slides in the presentation is displayed and you can select which slide you want the presentation to open with – it need not be the first one in the list.

All that remains to be done is for the same process to be repeated to link each section back to the menu file.

TIP

Creating the 'Return to Menu' action button on the **Slide Master** of the children's presentations will mean that every slide will have a 'Return to Menu' button. When you copy an action button you also copy the 'instructions' that it contains, so copying the button and pasting it on each group's **Slide Master** will speed up the process.

A booklet, *Presentations and Interactive Multimedia Packages with Powerpoint* is available on the CD-ROM accompanying this book.

What will the children learn?

That information comes from a variety of sources and can be presented in a variety of forms

The number of sources and the range of forms that the children experience is one of the ways of adjusting the challenge of this task. Aim to increase the children's capability by introducing new media or sources.

That sounds convey information and that pictures provide information

While this may not be new learning for many children, the ease with which inappropriate Clip Art or meaningless sound effects can be added to *PowerPoint* slides makes this project a useful context with which to emphasise the way in which images and sounds can communicate scientific knowledge.

That computers use icons to provide information and instructions

Involving the children in the creation of a computer-based resource for others to use will help them to consider the use of icons and how we 'read' them.

To use ICT appropriately to communicate ideas through text

Part of the appropriate use of ICT involves employing the provisional nature of the technology to explore effects and layout as well as experimenting with phrases to clarify understanding and meaning. Using the technology to 'type up' previously planned and corrected text is therefore missing out on some of the key benefits of the software. Encourage the children to use the spell-check reminders and thesaurus to extend their vocabulary. Facilities such as cut and paste and dragging text to reorder it exploit the potential of computer-based writing.

To select and use different techniques to communicate ideas through pictures

The important learning in this project is the appropriateness of the technique in relation to the idea. For example: duplicating and flipping over elements of pictures to provide symmetrical images; using simple line drawings to clarify; capturing detail with digital microscope or camera images; using video to show dynamic events or frames from video to capture fast-moving action.

That ICT can be used to capture and present sounds

The usefulness of presenting short clips that can be reproduced time and time again at the click of a button can be compared with other methods of recording and playback.

To use ICT to organise, reorganise and analyse ideas and information

It is important to ensure that there is enough time for children to evaluate and make changes to their work. Look out for opportunities to add a section missed out in the original planning or possibly add links to connect slides produced by different groups which relate to each other.

That a screen image can be a finished product

Emphasise here that there is no point printing out the slides because they will not 'work'.

To select suitable information and media and prepare it for processing using ICT

If time allows, compare different methods of preparing media, e.g. scanning a pencil drawing or making a computer-based drawing.

To use a multimedia authoring program to organise, refine and present information in different forms for a specific audience

Deciding on the audience and their needs is an important part of this project. Producing a resource for younger children, about the birds that visit the feeders, for example, can be a valuable way to encourage the authors to explain carefully and use images appropriately.

Challenging the more able and supporting the less able: modifying the project for older and younger pupils

Both the complexity and the scale of this project can be adapted to provide a suitable level of challenge for all children. In addition to the new media and techniques which the project affords there are plenty of opportunities for less able children to revisit and refine previously introduced skills, techniques and knowledge. By providing a presentation template different parts of the project can be partially prepared so that the tasks left for the children to complete are suitably challenging for them, and laborious or inappropriate tasks removed.

To increase the challenge a greater range of media can be required of some groups and able children can be involved in the structuring and creation of the class resource which connects all the different sections together. Rather than use existing resources, they can also be encouraged and supported to create original sound and movie files. A further way of challenging some children is by suggesting that those who have mastered the techniques create a multiple-choice quiz with action buttons to provide feedback. By providing a creative challenge, the ICT techniques that they have learnt can be applied and any scientific misconceptions can be revealed and addressed.

Why teach this?

As an integrated project it covers the breadth of the ICT NC KS2 PoS very well. Through finding things out, developing ideas and communicating and sharing them, elements of statements 1a–c, 2a and 3a, 3b can all be addressed. The opportunity to discuss the strengths and weaknesses of the use of ICT for creating this type of information source does not happen automatically but it can make a valuable contribution to the 'Reviewing, modifying and evaluating work as it progresses' strand of the ICT PoS if the opportunities are planned.

Both the real scientific information and the real audience make this a purposeful context to develop aspects of ICT capability covered in the QCA ICT Scheme of Work Units 3A: *Combining text and graphics*, 3B: *Manipulating sound* and 4A: *Writing for different audiences*. The scientific context also helps to provide real reasons for incorporating a wide variety of media.

The activity makes a novel use of presentation software to support teaching and learning of almost any science topic. The children's level of science understanding can be developed and assessed through the process of representing their scientific knowledge using ICT. Putting children in the role of teacher demonstrating their understanding for younger children is an effective way to help them articulate what they have learnt. With a little ingenuity it is possible to design a brief for an information source of this type to enhance any of the QCA scheme of work units.

See also *Humanities* Project 5 (*Repurposing information for different audiences*), *Humanities* Project 8 (*Making an information source*) and *English* Project 9 (*Creating an information website*) for related activities.

Project Fact Card: Project 8: Digital video – freeze frame

Who is it for?

- 7- to 10-year-olds (NC Levels 2–9)

What will the children do?

- Use a digital camcorder to film an investigation which is then analysed frame by frame on the computer to make visible an event which happens too fast for accurate observation

What should the children know already?

- Previous use of cameras is helpful but not essential
- That images can be captured and stored in a digital camera
- That images captured by a camera can be transferred to a computer via a lead, and can be viewed on screen

What do I need to know?

- How to use your digital camcorder to film an experiment
- How to connect your camcorder to the computer
- How to operate the software to view and analyse the video that you have captured
- How to capture individual frames from a video
- How to time events using a video camera

What resources will I need?

- Digital video camera or camcorder
- Digital video-editing software

What will the children learn?

- How to record and edit video and view a frame at a time
- That information comes from a variety of sources and can be presented in a variety of forms
- That pictures provide information
- To use ICT to test a hypothesis
- That it is important to interpret information and to understand it
- That video can be used to identify patterns and relationships
- That video can be used to monitor changes in environmental conditions
- That a video can be used to take samples of data for a set period of time
- To identify opportunities and design simple investigations for which the collection of data through a computer device is both feasible and advantageous

How to challenge the more able

- Encourage independent use of the camera and software
- Provide opportunities to design their own investigation using a camcorder

How to support the less able

- Set up the camera for use
- Assist with connecting the camera to the computer and loading the software

Why teach this?

- The project contributes to section 1 of the ICT NC KS2 PoS, 'Finding things out', through the capture and interpretation of visual information. It also teaches children how to share information described in statement 3a. Discussion about the effectiveness of this method of collecting and sharing information required by the 'Reviewing, modifying and evaluating work as it progresses' strand of the ICT PoS contributes to the value of the learning.
- Elements of the content of QCA ICT Scheme of Work Units 5F and 6A are covered by this project.
- Digital video is a powerful tool for primary science teachers and learners to extend the range of investigative skills described in the science National Curriculum Sc1 section 2. A project of this sort can enhance many of the QCA scheme of work units – from the slow movement of shadows in Unit 3F to the rapid vibration of instruments in Unit 5F.

PROJECT 8

Digital video – freeze frame

What will the children do?

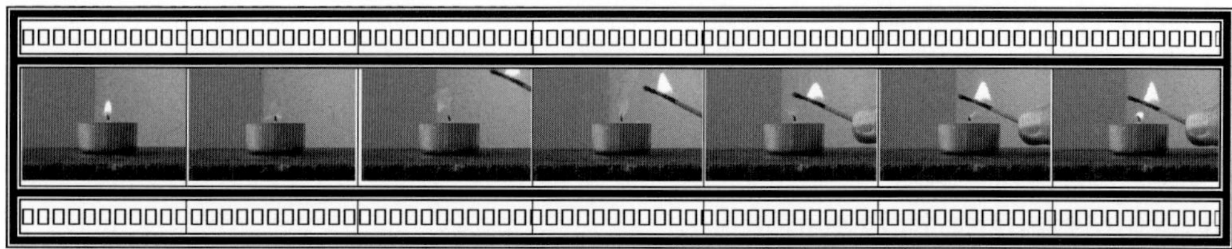

Looking at the relighting of a candle frame by frame shows that the flame does not touch the wick before it relights

Digital video makes images like the sequence above accessible to primary teachers and children. All the functions that we have come to expect of a word processor – cut, copy, paste, insert – and many more are available once the digitised video format exported from digital camcorders is transferred to a computer.

Activity 1: Capturing the action

Start by filming an event that requires careful observation, like the relighting of a candle shown above, and pose questions about what is happening (e.g. what is burning and whether or not the match touched the wick before the candle relit). By connecting the camera to the computer and interactive whiteboard the scene can be replayed frame by frame to help the children answer the questions. The value of the camera in assisting observation is then discussed and the children begin to plan their own investigation that could benefit from being filmed and analysed in a similar way.

Activity 2: Video observation

The children film and view their video using the computer to help to interpret what they have observed and answer their questions. Frames from the video are captured and saved to be used in their report.

What should the children know already?

Previous use of cameras is helpful but not essential

With the advent of Liquid Crystal Display (LCD) screens the framing of camera shots has become much easier. The co-ordination required to aim and operate a camera will be developed though this activity, but the greater the proficiency that the children have in this area, the more time can be devoted to the science and the interpretation of the information. The majority of scientific investigations can be filmed using a small tripod or placing the camera firmly on a table.

That images can be captured and stored in a digital camera

Any doubt that the children may have about the reliability of the technology to faithfully capture images of an event should be dispelled through the demonstration. The children should be familiar with the idea that computer images are recorded as numbers and that any storage medium has a finite capacity.

That images captured by a camera can be transferred to a computer via a lead, and can be viewed on screen

Drawing the children's attention to their previous use of digital cameras or any other peripheral equipment, printers or scanners, for example, will help them to recognise similarities with the process of downloading video information from the camcorder to the computer.

What do I need to know?

How to use your digital camcorder to film an experiment

There is no substitute for reading the manual that came with your camcorder and experimenting. There are three key things that you will need to check:

1. That you have a tape or other storage medium inserted correctly and, in the case of tape, cued in the right place.
2. That the camcorder is switched to 'camera' (record) not 'VCR' (video cassette recorder or playback). Test it by pressing record – the light or indicator in the LCD should display that recording is in progress. Switch to VCR to rewind and view your test. REMEMBER to switch back to camera!

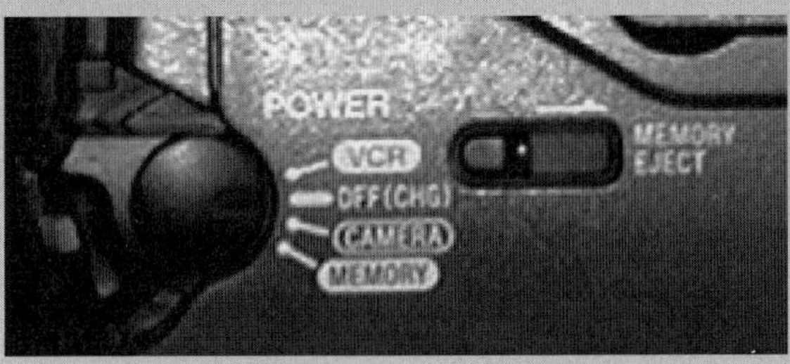

3. That the shot is framed in the view finder or LCD. Use the camera position and the zoom, if you have one, to make sure that what you can see is clear.

How to connect your camcorder to the computer

Again the manual is called for, as you will usually need to install the software supplied with the camera before connecting to the computer for the first time. Once the software is installed you may find that the camera needs to be set to download before it is connected via the lead supplied to the USB port on the computer. After connecting, wait a while for the computer to recognise the camera and indicate that it is ready for use – the **Add Hardware Wizard** may be activated at this point; follow instructions on the screen if necessary.

How to operate the software to view and analyse the video that you have captured

With the camera connected to the computer the recorded video images can be downloaded to the computer. The software that supports the Digital Blue cameras downloads the video as files – a separate one for each clip. With more sophisticated cameras which have tapes, software like Apple's *iMovie* or Pixela's *ImageMixer* for Sony cameras allows the tape controls to be operated from the computer screen. As well as rewinding, fast forward, play, stop and pause facilities, buttons are available to progress or rewind the footage a frame at a time.

How to capture individual frames from a video

Most software will also have a snapshot tool which will enable a single frame to be saved as a still image or photograph. Stop or pause the video at the frame that you require; using the frame-by-frame buttons the precise moment that you require can be frozen in the display window. Clicking on the snapshot tool – the centre button at the bottom in the *ImageMixer* screen above – will cause the current frame to be captured and saved as a separate file. Some software will add the captured image to a clipboard or gallery first from where it can be exported or saved.

How to time events using a video camera

One of the additional benefits of using a video camera to gather data is that the camera's timer can be used to measure intervals or provide precise timings. There are several ways to record time using a digital video camera and software. The simplest, if using a camera without time codes, could be to add a stop watch to the shot so that the time is visible alongside the event. When the video is analysed frame by frame the time at which different events occurred can be observed in the frame.

With some cameras it is possible to display the date and time at the bottom of the LCD screen during playback so that when reviewing video in the camera the time that the picture was taken is recorded. Refer to the camera manual for how to display the time and date data if they do not appear by default.

Most software will also contain a time display; in *ImageMixer* the display shows hour: minute: second: frame (full motion video captures 25 frames each second so each frame represents 4/100ths of a second).

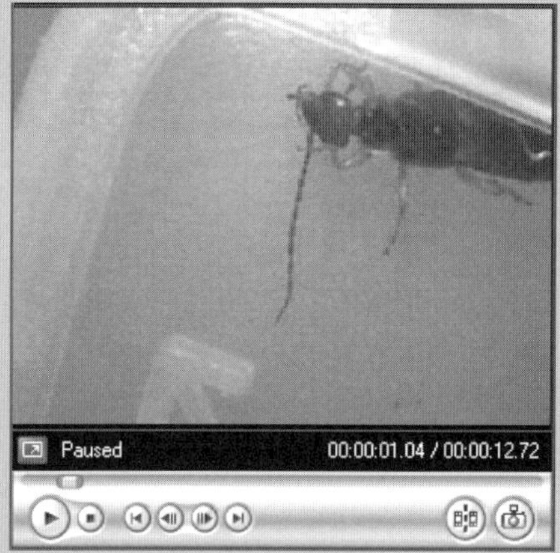

Windows Movie Maker, which comes as part of the Accessories with Windows XP, records hundredths of a second and so jumps .04 of a second each frame.

Digital Blue Movie Creator runs at 15 frames a second so, although no time code is displayed, measurements between events can be calculated by counting frames.

What will the children learn?

How to record and edit video and view a frame at a time

Children are thrilled to see their own video images on the screen. Their motivation, coupled with considerable experience of watching moving images and understanding the medium, makes this task not as complicated as you might first think.

That information comes from a variety of sources and can be presented in a variety of forms

The careful step-by-step analysis of an event that took place in less than a second shows the children how information can be extracted from moving images. Using a snapshot from the video in their report also extends the range of ways in which they can present information.

That pictures provide information

The careful observation of changes between frames highlights what pictures can tell us.

To use ICT to test a hypothesis

Using the children's explanations of what they think is happening when observing any quickly changing dynamic event at first hand, hypotheses can be developed that video analysis can help to test.

That it is important to interpret information and to understand it

Even hard evidence from 'caught on camera' freeze frames does not explain what is going on in an event. Encourage children to offer several explanations of what is happening and why.

That video can be used to identify patterns and relationships

By exporting frames from different stages in a process and placing them side by side, similarities and differences can be identified and discussed.

That video can be used to monitor changes in environmental conditions

Showing the children some webcams will help them to interpret information about what is happening in different parts of the world. By capturing data in this way the camera is monitoring changes that happen very quickly. Repeated use over time or time-lapse filming can enable changes in conditions to be identified.

That a video can be used to take samples of data for a set period of time

Some video cameras can be set up to make the same sort of time-lapse videos that were described in Project 2. The interval recording function switches on the camera for one second every hour so that events that would take too long to observe (for example, flowers opening or puddles evaporating) can be captured and better understood.

To identify opportunities and design simple investigations for which the collection of data through a computer device is both feasible and advantageous

Through carrying out their investigation children will recognise the benefits and practical limitations of digital video so that they can make informed decisions about when, and when not, to employ this technology to aid their investigations.

Challenging the more able and supporting the less able: modifying the project for older and younger pupils

Once the camera has been set up for use, the pressing of a button is all that is required to start and stop the video recording, and all children can participate to some extent. Some children may get confused by the different modes or functions of the camera, however, and forget to switch between VCR for playing back and Camera to record. A level of support can be achieved by making the children work in twos, with one targeting the camera and the other checking the LCD screen or recording light. Alternatively use the cheaper Digital Blue cameras, which are designed for children at Key Stages 1 and 2 and are very simple to operate so that the children can be independent.

While it is possible to have the camera connected and the software running to avoid problems during a lesson, we need to be careful that learning opportunities are not avoided at the same time. Assist children appropriately, according to need, with connecting the camera to the computer and loading the software. Once connected, most software is very visual and only a few buttons are needed to view and analyse the captured video.

Children who are proficient with ICT should be encouraged to use the camera and software independently. For some children an additional challenge may be appropriate – saving snapshots from the film and inserting them in word-processing or paint software in order to add a commentary or labels, for example. The real proof of understanding, both scientific and technological, is the ability to apply their knowledge and understanding to answer their own enquiry. Provide opportunities for more able children to design their own investigations using a camcorder.

Why teach this?

Digital video has put the filming and editing of moving images within the grasp of primary children. The control afforded by the technology makes scientific events, which happen too quickly or too slowly, readily observable. The project contributes to section 1 of the ICT NC KS2 PoS, 'Finding things out', through the capture and interpretation of visual information. Although video images are not always viewed as data, the information that can be gained with video-assisted observation helps children to understand how ICT can be used to find things out. The fact that children have seen the event 'live' makes the activity a more powerful learning experience than watching a pre-recorded video. It also teaches children another way to share information described in statement 3a of the ICT PoS. Discussion about the effectiveness of this method of collecting and sharing information required by the 'Reviewing, modifying and evaluating work as it progresses' strand of the ICT PoS contributes to the value of the learning.

The activity relates to elements of the content of the following QCA ICT scheme of work units:

- 5F: *Monitoring environmental conditions and changes*, as there are similarities in the set-up of data-logging equipment and the video, particularly for time-lapse filming;
- 6A: *Multimedia presentation*, as evidence from the video could be used in a presentation and the activity extends the children's understanding of the range of ICT media available and their use.

Digital video is a powerful tool for both primary science teachers and learners. The ability to slow down or speed up observations to capture patterns or observe phenomena extends the range of investigative skills that the science National Curriculum Sc1 section 2 is aiming to develop. An activity of this sort can enhance many of the QCA scheme of work units – from the slow movement of shadows in Unit 3F: *Light and shadows* to the rapid vibration of instruments in Unit 5F: *Changing sounds*. Aim to use the technology enough for the children to understand its potential, but not too much, so that there are opportunities for the children to decide when an investigation would benefit from video analysis.

See also *English* Project 4 (*Working with audio*), *English* Project 7 (*Photo-dramas*), *English* Project 8 (*Digital video*), *Humanities* Project 9 (*A video of a visit to a place of worship*) and *Art* Project 10 (*Creating a digital 'silent film'*) for related activities.

Project Fact Card: Project 9: Data logging

Who is it for?

- 9- to 11-year-olds (NC Levels 3–5)

What will the children do?

- Using sensors connected to a computer with data-logging software, children predict, record and analyse changes in temperature, sound or light that occur during an investigation

What should the children know already?

- How to select tools by clicking on buttons
- How to click and drag and right click
- Familiarity with tape recorder button icons

What do I need to know?

- How to connect a data logger and sensors to a computer
- How to set up graphing software to display data in real time and begin logging
- How to pause a graph and enable children to predict readings
- How to label predictions and display actual results
- How to save, copy and print graphs

What resources will I need?

- Data logger and sensors
- Data-logging software

What will the children learn?

- That information can be presented in a variety of forms and collected from a variety of sources
- That data represented graphically can be easier to understand than textual data
- That information can be represented as graphs but that this can only provide limited answers to questions
- That ICT can be used to store and sort information
- That line graphs can be used to show continuously changing information
- To interpret and analyse information in graphs
- To use ICT to test a hypothesis
- To work with others to interpret information
- That sensing devices can be used to monitor changes in environmental conditions
- That a device attached to a computer can take readings of conditions such as light intensity, temperature and sound levels
- That a computer can take samples of data for a set period of time
- To identify opportunities and design simple investigations for which the collection of data through a computer device is both feasible and advantageous
- That computers can monitor physical factors

How to challenge the more able

- Encourage independent operation of the software
- Encourage adaptation of investigation or other uses of the technology

How to support the less able

- Provide additional experience of observing data capture while altering the condition of the sensors
- Set up the graphing software with the children

Why teach this?

- Through data logging, a range of elements of the ICT NC KS2 PoS statements is addressed. It develops understanding of the ways that ICT can help to find things out, using appropriate sources and interpreting the information – 1a–c. It also shows how ICT can monitor external conditions (2b) and provides opportunity to discuss the strengths and weaknesses of the use of ICT for data logging as outlined in 4b in the 'Reviewing, modifying and evaluating work as it progresses' strand of the ICT PoS. Discussing comparisons with environmental monitoring carried out in the wider community will add to the breadth of study.
- The project can prepare for and extend the content of QCA ICT Scheme of Work Units 5C, 5E, 5F and 6C.
- Data logging is an explicit requirement of the National Curriculum – Sc1, 2f. As well as recording a log or graph most software will also display a live meter reading to help teaching demonstrations. QCA Scheme of Work Units 4C, 5D and 5F could benefit from the type of activity described in this project.

PROJECT 9

Data logging

What will the children do?

Data-logging equipment and software is used in all branches of science to enable continuous monitoring of experimental conditions. An understanding of the processes involved in taking careful readings using thermometers and producing graphs with and without ICT will help the children to appreciate the automatic sensing, recording and presentation of readings that data-logging technology undertakes. The first activity involves using the technology as an interactive teaching aid with the whole class, ideally with an interactive whiteboard. In groups, the children will then go on to set up the equipment for their own investigations. Most data-logging equipment will come with light, heat and sound sensors as standard so a range of investigations can be undertaken. Investigations which involve comparisons between the temperatures of two melting ice blocks in different conditions, for example, can be carried out with additional plug-in sensors. Data Harvest's Easy Sense Q3 used in this example can have two additional sensors plugged into the interface, making it possible to monitor three different temperatures simultaneously.

Activity 1: Logging together

Remote sensors connected to the Easy Sense Q3

Set up the data-logging equipment with two probes in different conditions – one in a thermos flask and the other in a bicycle bottle, for example. Put the same amount of chilled or warm drink in each and begin to log the two temperatures, displaying the graph on the screen.

After the children have discussed predictions and observed the graph that is being plotted on the screen for a while, press pause on the graph. Although the graph pauses, the software will continue to monitor the temperatures. Invite children to draw how they think the line will continue for each sensor and ask them to justify and label their predictions. Data Harvest's Sensing Science Primary *Graph* software has a facility to draw predictions and add text labels to the graph while it is paused. It is also possible to use the whiteboard software to draw over the top of a graph on the screen.

Once sufficient time has elapsed to cover the predictions that the children have made, pressing the pause button again will reveal the readings that have been taken in the meantime. Discussions about the children's expectations, the reliability of the technology, ways that the sensors can be checked, reasons for the differences between the two liquids and the fairness of the test can all contribute to valuable science and ICT learning.

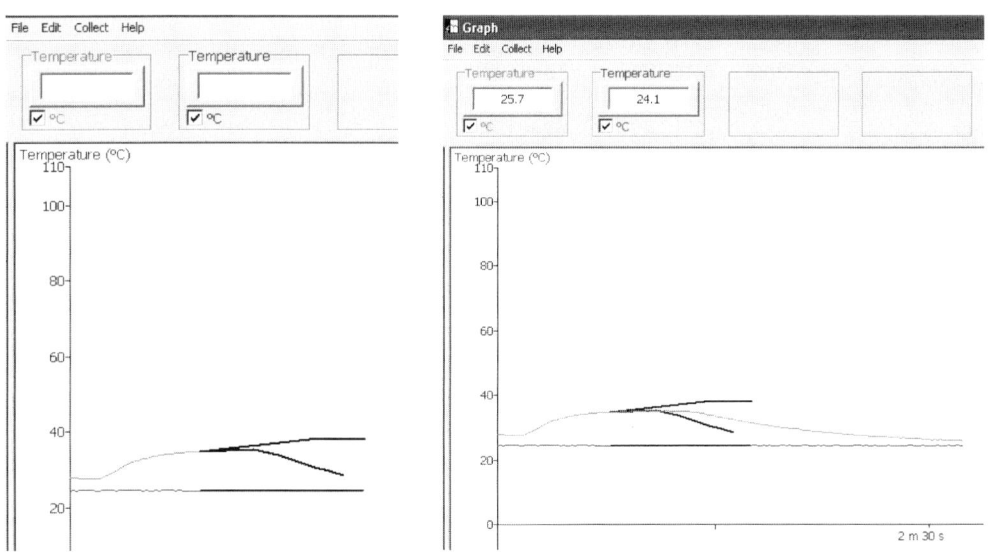

Once predictions have been made, the actual reading can be revealed

Activity 2: Designing data-logging investigations

Once the children have an understanding of the way the software and the interface and sensors are set up, they can use the equipment in their own scientific enquiry. Which sensors to monitor and the duration can be set up using the software. Testing insulation to keep drinks at the desired temperature or testing sound insulation using the sound sensor are both possible. The light sensor can be used to monitor conditions in the classroom out of school hours or changes to output from a bulb in an electrical circuit when the circuit is altered or reflectors added, for example. The extent to which the children take responsibility for the setting up of the equipment can be varied to meet the learning needs of the groups involved.

What should the children know already?

This could be the children's first experience of sense and control equipment being connected to the computer. Explaining how the sensors are connected and the communication that takes place via the leads will help. Draw parallels with other equipment that they may have experienced, like the digital microscope, and the way that it could be controlled with the computer.

How to select tools by clicking on buttons

Instructions are given through buttons and menus in ways that are similar to most current software and children can draw on their previous experience to help them to use the data-logging software.

How to click and drag and right click

These familiar ways of operating the mouse or whiteboard will be useful for these tasks. Predictions are made using a similar function to most polygon drawing tools where each mouse click plots a new point which is joined to the previous one by a line. A right click ends the line.

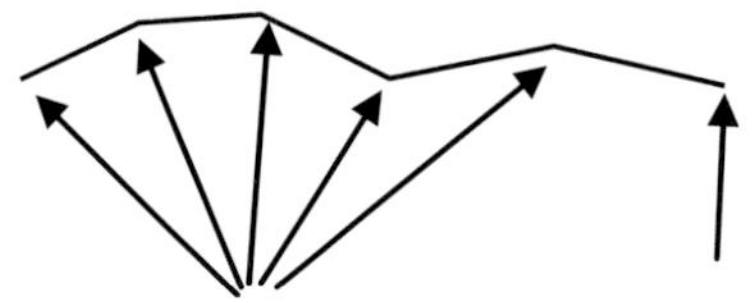

Familiarity with tape recorder button icons

The start, stop and pause/resume instructions for plotting data are given by clicking on icons similar to tape and CD controls.

What do I need to know?

How to connect a data logger and sensors to a computer

Most data-logging equipment comes with an interface which is connected to the computer via a lead. It is usual for the software to need installing on the computer before the interface is plugged in for the first time. The majority of peripherals – the term used for equipment plugged into the computer – now use the USB ports.

Connect the USB lead to the data logger and the computer and connect any additional sensors that you intend to use. Using a mains supply to the data logger, if one is available, will save using the batteries. If the data logger is not connected properly a message will be displayed when you launch the data-logging software.

How to set up graphing software to display data in real time and begin logging

In Data Harvest's Sensing Science Primary *Graph* software, the screen will open with an empty graph.

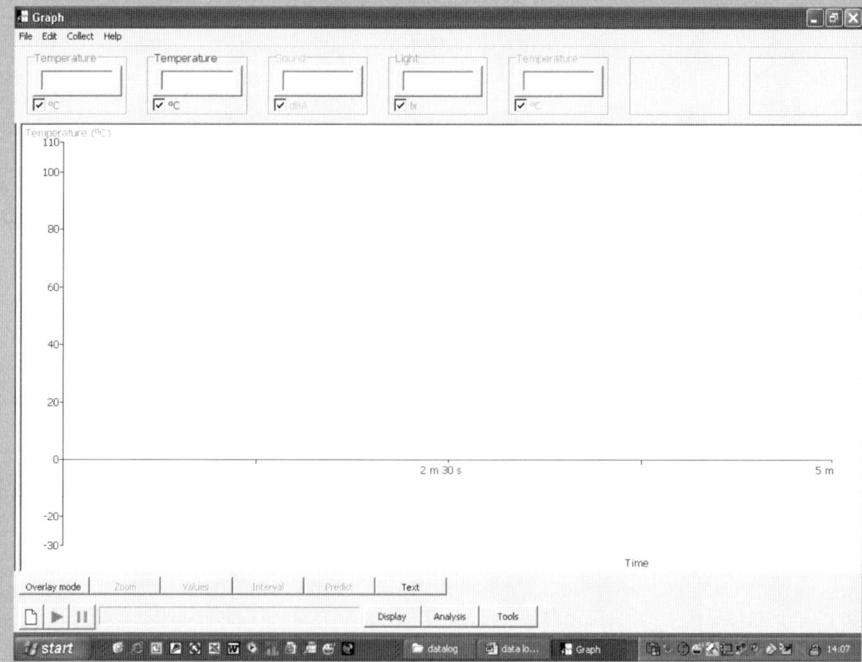

Data Harvest's Sensing Science Primary Graph *software (Sensing Science screenshot courtesy of Data Harvest, www.data-harvest.co.uk)*

It is possible to gather simple recordings by ticking only the sensors that you wish to monitor at the top of the screen and pressing ▶ in the bottom left of the screen to start logging.

To make further choices click on the **New** icon () in the bottom left of the screen. The **Recording Wizard** window will appear and choices about the type of logging that you wish to carry out, the timespan and the interval or sample rate can be chosen.

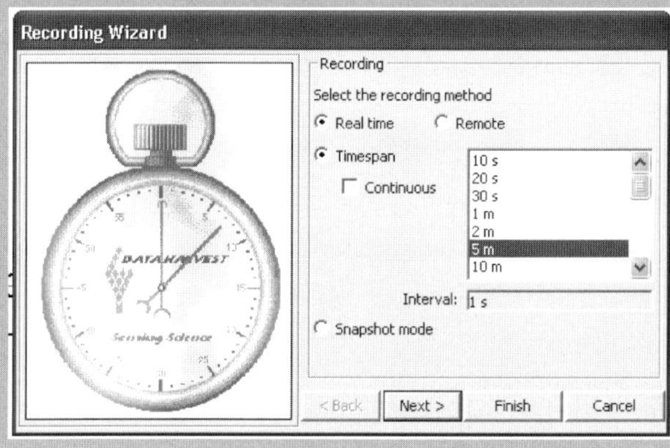

Select **Real time** for using the data logger attached to the computer and viewing results as they happen. The **Remote** option is for setting up the data logger to capture data once it has been disconnected from the computer. Data are stored in the unit to be collected the next time it is connected. The 'Timespan' selected will dictate the scale on the horizontal axis and for how long readings will be taken. Clicking **Continuous** will make the monitoring continue until you click stop. The scale on the horizontal access will change each time the graph reaches the end. The Interval displays the sample rate, or how often readings are taken. The longer the 'timespan' required for the experiment the greater the interval will become; if you wanted to record for a month, for example, readings would only be taken every hour.

Selecting **Snapshot mode** allows readings to be gathered at times determined by clicking on the graph. Each time the graph is clicked a set of bars appears to signify the readings from each selected sensor at that time.

Selecting **Next** produces the **Sensor Wizard** window, which enables the sensors that you wish to monitor to be chosen. The three built-in sensors (3, 4 and 5) can be selected or de-selected and any plug-in sensors are identified. If you plug in new sensors, clicking **Re-Detect** should identify what is attached to each sensor port.

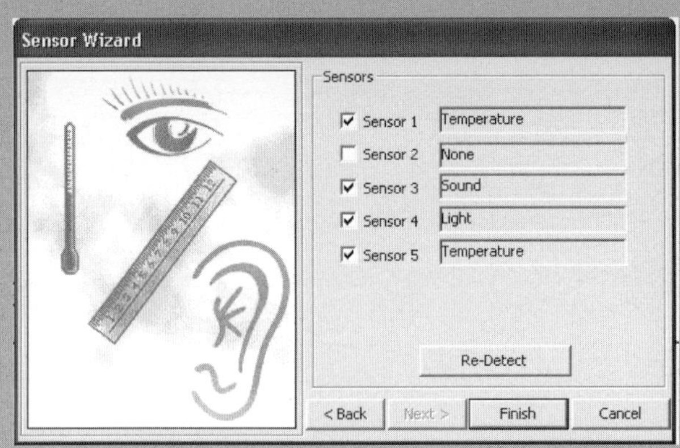

How to pause a graph and enable children to predict readings

In order to be able to pause the graph and discuss what will happen to the readings, the 'timespan' setting needs to be great enough to allow some observation before the graph is paused and time for discussion. With the graph set up to record and logging in progress, press the **Pause** button.

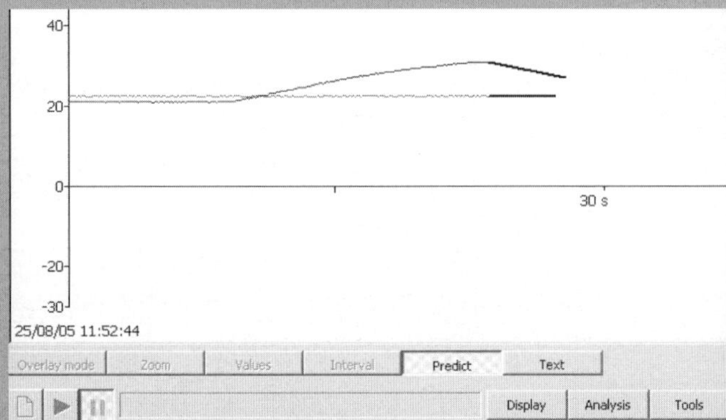

Clicking on **Predict** and moving the mouse back to the graph will cause a movable black line to appear where the plotting is paused. Children can be asked to draw how they think the trace will continue by positioning the line and clicking with the mouse – or pen on the whiteboard – each time they think that the line will change direction. A right click on the mouse ends their prediction. Clicking on **Predict** again will start a new prediction line for another child to suggest his/her idea for the same sensor. To switch to another sensor's plot line click anywhere to the left of the vertical (Y) axis and click on **Predict** again.

How to label predictions and display actual results

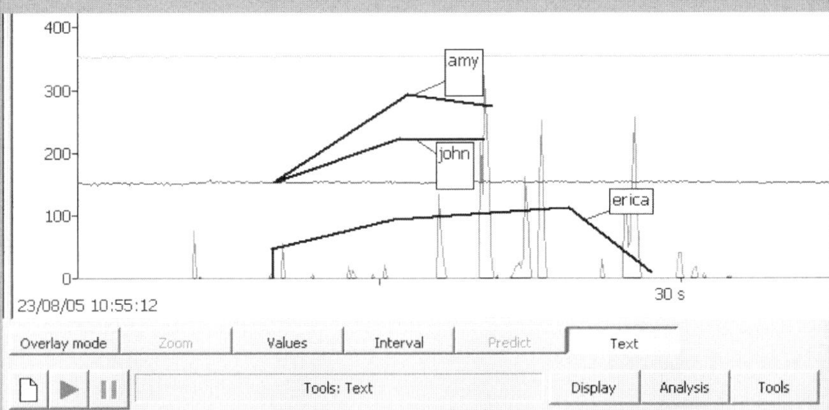

If multiple predictions are added, labels will help to identify different suggestions. Adding text in this way can also be useful in identifying particular events when conditions were changed in an experiment. To add text, click on the **Text** button and then click the place on the graph that you wish to label. A dialogue box will appear where you can type the text required.

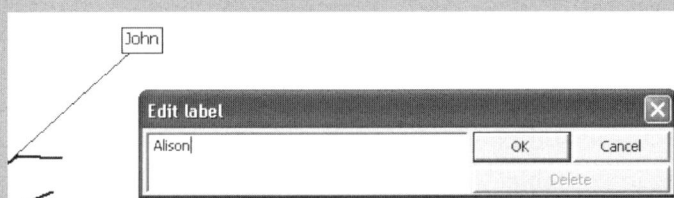

Clicking **OK** presents a rectangle that can be positioned on the graph and placed by clicking the mouse. A line will appear between the text box and the position of the first mouse click which identified the place that you wished to label. With the **Text** button depressed, labels can be repositioned by clicking and dragging, or edited and deleted by double clicking on them. To stop editing text, click the **Text** button again.

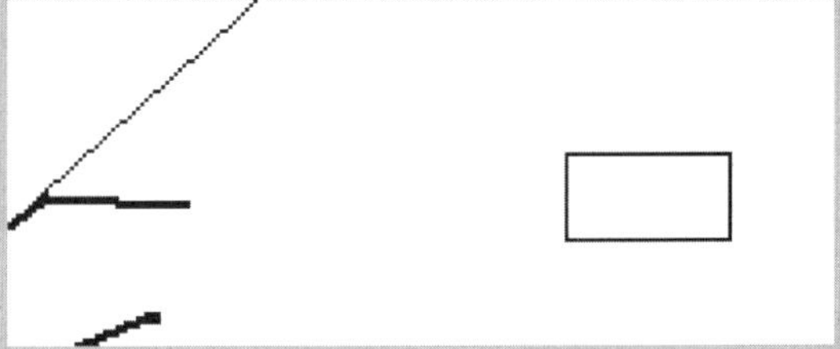

Once predictions and labels are in place the actual readings taken by the data logger can be revealed by pressing the **Pause/Continue** button once more. If the 'Timespan' set has elapsed, the graph will be completed; if not, the graph will continue to be plotted.

How to save, copy and print graphs

Save in data-logging software will usually save the data – that is, the numbers that have been recorded. Sensing Science Primary *Graph* software enables a graph to be saved by selecting **Save Meta File . . .** from the **File** menu; the graph to be copied for pasting into another piece of software by selecting **Copy Graph** from the **Edit** menu; or the graph to be printed by selecting **Print Graph . . .** from the **File** menu.

What will the children learn?

As well as learning about the capabilities of data-logging hardware and software, the automatic functions of the technology provide the children with access to well-presented data relating to their own classroom investigations. Using ICT to support the time-consuming processes of measuring, recording and presenting the data enables the teaching and learning to focus on the higher order skills of interpreting and analysing the information.

That information can be presented in a variety of forms and collected from a variety of sources

This activity should extend the range of sources with which the children are familiar. Pointing out the usefulness of automatic remote monitoring provided by weather and air quality services, for example, will develop their ability to compare their own work with applications outside school.

That data represented graphically can be easier to understand than textual data

Dragging the left margin of the Sensing Science Primary *Graph* software to the right will reveal the numerical data in a table. Searching for readings when sensors were equal, for example, is easier on the graph than the table. The **Values** button will allow you to identify individual readings on the graph which are simultaneously highlighted in the table.

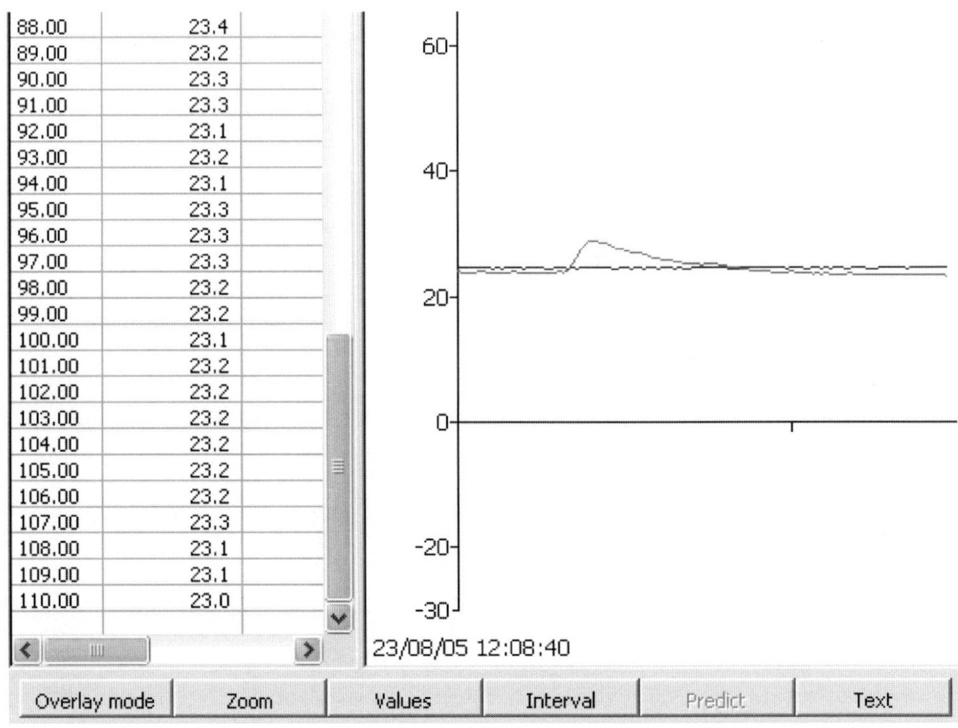

88.00	23.4
89.00	23.2
90.00	23.3
91.00	23.3
92.00	23.1
93.00	23.2
94.00	23.1
95.00	23.3
96.00	23.3
97.00	23.3
98.00	23.2
99.00	23.2
100.00	23.1
101.00	23.2
102.00	23.2
103.00	23.2
104.00	23.2
105.00	23.2
106.00	23.2
107.00	23.3
108.00	23.1
109.00	23.1
110.00	23.0

Data Harvest's Sensing Science Primary Graph *software with data revealed (Sensing Science screenshot courtesy of Data Harvest, www.data-harvest.co.uk)*

That information can be represented as graphs but that this can only provide limited answers to questions

The data-logging software provides graphs that children can look at objectively. Encouraging children to offer alternative explanations for readings on the graph will help to show that the graph is not the answer.

That ICT can be used to store and sort information

Saving sets of data and returning to them in a later lesson for further analysis reinforces the value of capturing information in this format.

That line graphs can be used to show continuously changing information

The live plotting of the data which responds to changes that are made to the sensors is a powerful demonstration of the way that graphs can represent changing circumstances.

To interpret and analyse information in graphs

Making sense of the stories that graphs can tell is central to this activity. Asking children to explain graphs which they have not created – like the one below, which plots the light, sound and temperature of the dawn – can further develop their ability to analyse.

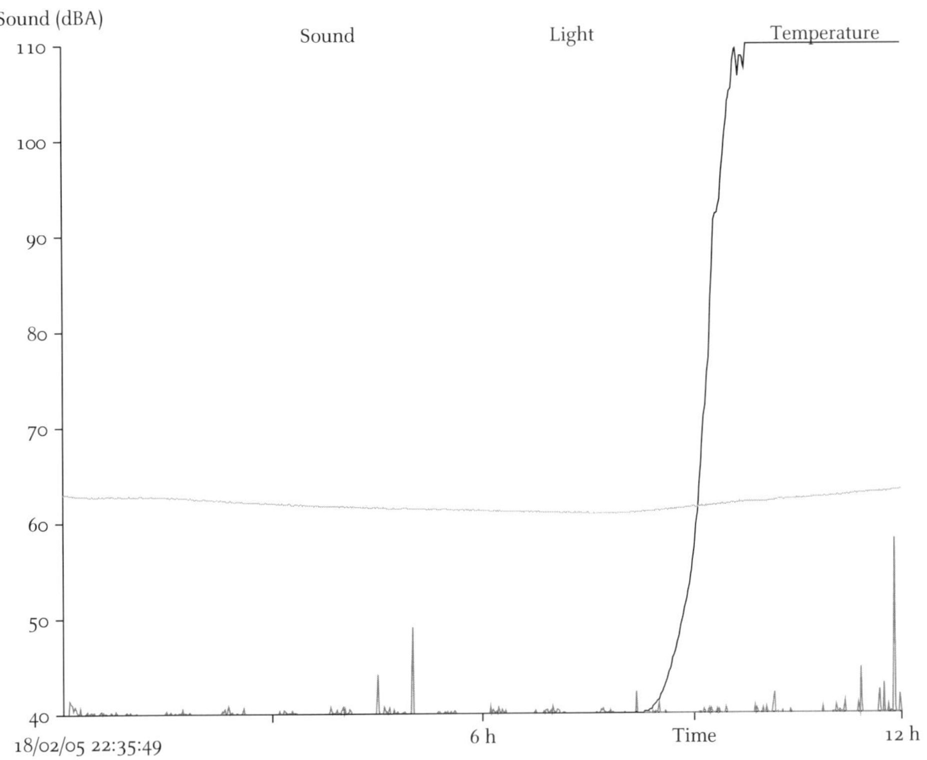

To use ICT to test a hypothesis

The way that children can record predictions and explain their reasons provides good ICT and science learning opportunities.

To work with others to interpret information

Through recording their predictions and comparing contrasting viewpoints the collaborative nature of the activity helps to develop the ability to interpret information.

That sensing devices can be used to monitor changes in environmental conditions

Using sensors to monitor whether the chicks will be warm enough in the classroom overnight or other questions that can be answered by environmental monitoring helps children to recognise the value of the technology.

That a device attached to a computer can take readings of conditions such as light intensity, temperature and sound levels

While temperature is easily measured in primary classrooms, the addition of light and sound sensors opens the way to other types of science investigation or visualising the dynamics of pieces of music even.

That a computer can take samples of data for a set period of time

Involving the children in setting up the data logger, either for remote sensing or in real time, will help them understand how it works and how they can use it.

To identify opportunities and design simple investigations for which the collection of data through a computer device is both feasible and advantageous

Ultimately the aim is for the children to be able to make informed decisions of how the data logger may assist with the design and conduct of their investigations.

That computers can monitor physical factors

The understanding that computers can, through an interface, sense changes in the 'real world' is important learning.

Challenging the more able and supporting the less able: modifying the project for older and younger pupils

Younger or less experienced learners may require more time 'playing' with the equipment to see how changes that they make to the sensors are reflected in the graph displayed on the computer screen. It is also possible to display live meters with this software. Consider showing the meters prior to introducing the graphing software.

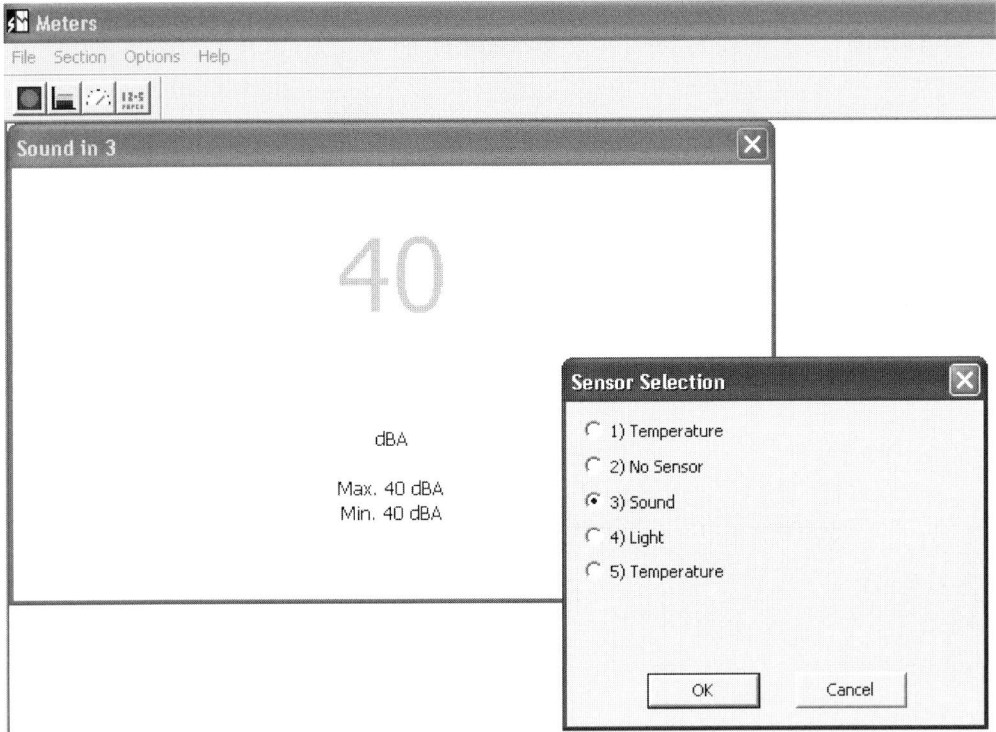

By providing additional experience of observing the capture and display of data, while altering the condition of the sensors, children begin to see the way the software functions and develop their ability to 'read' the graph. Once the class activity has been completed, some children will need additional assistance to set up the graphing software for their own investigation.

Able children can be encouraged to operate the software independently, making choices about the sensors and the time scale that their investigation requires. Some children will be able to recognise the potential benefit of the data logger and design other investigations. Challenge those who are capable to find out about how the technology is used in the wider world to monitor and capture data.

Why teach this?

As well as being a core requirement for scientific enquiry, the automatic functions of computer data logging provide scaffolding for young scientists to focus on the data and what they mean rather than be distracted by processing and presenting them. Through data logging, a range of elements of the ICT NC KS2 PoS statements is addressed. It develops understanding of the ways that ICT can help to find things out, using appropriate sources and interpreting the information described in statements 1a–c of the NC PoS. It also shows how ICT can monitor external conditions (2b in the KS2 PoS) and provides opportunity to discuss the strengths and weaknesses of the use of ICT for data logging as outlined in 4b in the 'Reviewing, modifying and evaluating work as it progresses' strand of the ICT NC KS2 PoS. Discussing comparisons with environmental monitoring carried out in the wider community will add to the breadth of study and provide useful assessment opportunities.

The project can prepare for and extend the content of QCA ICT Scheme of Work Units 5C: *Evaluating information, checking accuracy and questioning plausibility*, 5E: *Controlling devices*, 5F: *Monitoring environmental conditions and changes* and 6C: *Control and monitoring – What happens when . . . ?*

Data logging is an explicit requirement of the National Curriculum – Sc1, 2f. As well as recording a log or graph most software will also display a live meter reading to help teaching demonstrations by letting the whole class see readings from sensors on the whiteboard while an investigation is proceeding. QCA Scheme of Work Units 4C: *Keeping warm*, 5D: *Changing state* and 5F: *Changing sounds* could benefit from the type of activity described in this project.

See also *Maths* Project 10 (*Statistical investigations 2*) for related activities.

Project Fact Card: Project 10: Using search engines

Who is it for?

- 9- to 11-year-olds (NC Levels 3–5)

What will the children do?

- Use internet search engines to explore a scientific topic. The children will learn about the advanced search functions that enable them to focus their search to best effect. Images and text from different web pages will be used to create their own project or presentation

What should the children know already?

- How to use a web browser to view web pages
- The process and purpose of 'cut, copy and paste'
- How to create a document using a publishing package or a presentation using presentation software

What do I need to know?

- How to restrict unsuitable content when searching the web
- How to locate and use the advance search features of an online search engine
- How to store web page locations in **Favorites** (*sic*)
- How to copy text from a web page
- How to copy images from a web page

What resources will I need?

- Internet connection
- Internet Explorer or other web browser
- *PowerPoint* or presentation software
- Word processor or desktop publishing (DTP) software

What will the children learn?

- That information can be presented in a variety of forms and collected from a variety of sources
- To use appropriate search techniques to find information
- That information can be connected in different ways at the same time
- To use the tools in online search engines to find out the answers to specific questions
- That searches can be carried out using more than one criterion
- To use complex searches to locate information
- To understand the importance of choosing keywords to find information

How to challenge the more able

- Challenge them to find specific pieces of information
- Encourage them to interpret and repurpose information gathered
- Encourage them to check the source and plausibility of information

How to support the less able

- Restrict their search to a single site's search engine
- Provide a 'treasure hunt' template for their topic with a finite number of pieces of information required

Why teach this?

- The project is targeted at section 1 of the ICT NC KS2 PoS, 'Finding things out'. It also helps the children to learn to develop their ideas in their project or presentation described in statement 2a and share the information with their peers in 3a and 3b of the PoS. The opportunity to discuss the strengths and weaknesses of the use of ICT for this type of searching as required by the 'Reviewing, modifying and evaluating work as it progresses' strand of the ICT PoS should not be missed.
- The project builds on the content of QCA ICT Scheme of Work Units 3C and 4A and extends Units 5B and 5C. The project provides a scientific context for Unit 6D.
- Depending on the topic, the project can contribute to children's knowledge and understanding in Sc2, 3 or 4. Sc1, 2h will be addressed through the use of ICT to communicate appropriately. The use of the internet to support teaching and learning can enhance and extend QCA Science scheme of work units such as 5E, 5D or 5F.

PROJECT 10

Using search engines

What will the children do?

The fact that there are vast numbers of up-to-date science resources available on the internet is both a boon and a drawback. The purpose of this project is to help children develop techniques and strategies that will help them to locate and use the information that they require among the plethora of websites purporting to contain scientific information. In the context of many science topics there is the opportunity for children to research and present information: about animals or birds, planets or meteorites, materials or elements. The tasks involve children using ICT to locate and save information which they then present to the class or others via a printed topic book or *PowerPoint* presentation.

Activity 1: Locating and saving web pages

Once you have discussed the importance of choosing keywords and demonstrated how to widen or narrow searches, the children use a suitably restricted search engine to locate information on the internet. The addresses of relevant web pages are added to the **Favorites** (*sic*) folder in Internet Explorer for later use.

Activity 2: Harvesting web resources

The children are shown how to save and transfer text and images from a web page to their topic file. They then access the pages that they located in the previous activity and begin to assemble the information needed for their topic.

Activity 3: Addressing the audience

Having a real purpose for the children's writing helps to focus their work and maintain quality. As printed 'hardcopy', groups of children could contribute to a class book or provide information booklets for younger children; as a *PowerPoint* presentation, the work could be presented to peers, the whole school or parents. Considering the needs of the audience, the information that the children have assembled is repurposed to help them clarify their knowledge and understanding of the topic. Tools such as a thesaurus can be employed to simplify or extent vocabulary.

What should the children know already?

How to use a web browser to view web pages

Previous experience of the convention of web browsing will help to prepare the children for these tasks. They should know how to use the **Back** button and recognise that underlined words are usually hyperlinks which can be clicked to navigate to other information. Understanding that each web page has a Uniform Resource Locator (URL) that appears as the 'page's address' at the top of the browser window can help to explain **Favorites** (*sic*).

The process and purpose of 'cut, copy and paste'

Children should have had experience of using these edit functions in their work before, both within a document and between applications. The children will further develop their understanding that because the clipboard holds information that is copied or cut and that paste will paste whatever is on the clipboard, ICT-based information is provisional and easily edited.

How to create a document using a publishing package or a presentation using presentation software

The more familiar the children are with the software that is going to produce their topic, the more they can concentrate on locating and evaluating the information.

What do I need to know?

Two booklets, 'Harvesting Web Resources' and 'Web Browsing with Internet Explorer and Managing Favourites' are available on the CD-ROM accompanying this book.

How to restrict unsuitable content when searching the web

The internet contains information of every type imaginable – and some which is beyond the imagination of most people. For that reason, letting children roam or browse at will can be as dangerous as leaving them in the backstreets of a major city. All schools have some form of filter system that will restrict access to unsuitable material, but as teachers we must know that it is working before embarking on this type of searching activity. As most filtering tools are automatic ,some scientific information can be screened out because of the vocabulary on the web page. It is worth checking that information that you want the children to access is available and talk to the IT service provider about adjusting controls for specific sites. Most search engines also have settings that will filter the results that they show.

SafeSearch ⦿ No filtering ○ Filter using SafeSearch

How to locate and use the advance search features of an online search engine

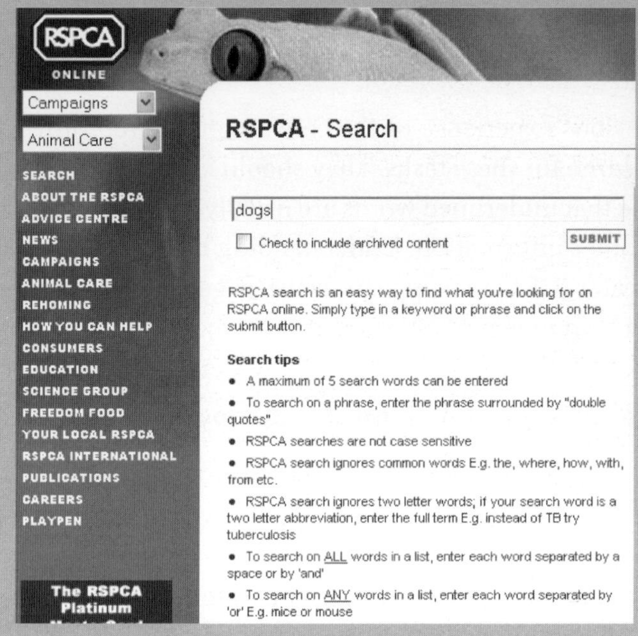
RSPCA
ONLINE
Campaigns
Animal Care
SEARCH
ABOUT THE RSPCA
ADVICE CENTRE
NEWS
CAMPAIGNS
ANIMAL CARE
REHOMING
HOW YOU CAN HELP
CONSUMERS
EDUCATION
SCIENCE GROUP
FREEDOM FOOD
YOUR LOCAL RSPCA
RSPCA INTERNATIONAL
PUBLICATIONS
CAREERS
PLAYPEN
The RSPCA Platinum
RSPCA - Search
dogs
Check to include archived content
SUBMIT
RSPCA search is an easy way to find what you're looking for on RSPCA online. Simply type in a keyword or phrase and click on the submit button.
Search tips
A maximum of 5 search words can be entered
To search on a phrase, enter the phrase surrounded by "double quotes"
RSPCA searches are not case sensitive
RSPCA search ignores common words E.g. the, where, how, with, from etc.
RSPCA search ignores two letter words; if your search word is a two letter abbreviation, enter the full term E.g. instead of TB try tuberculosis
To search on ALL words in a list, enter each word separated by a space or by 'and'
To search on ANY words in a list, enter each word separated by 'or' E.g. mice or mouse

A typical keyword search on an internet search engine will return hundreds of thousands of web pages in less than half a second. While most will sort the results with the most relevant first – using frequency of the keywords and their proximity to each other, for example – the more a search can be narrowed down, the greater our chances of success. The high profile of some internet search sites has made them household names, but it is worth trying a range of providers and use the one that suits you and your class the best. For some topics you may just want to search with a site using the search facility provided on the home page. The advantage is that the information will be relevant to the topic and some sites have advanced search facilities which enable search techniques to be taught.

monthly image
image gallery
information center
hubble art
search
Hubble Heritage Search Engine
Hubble Heritage Search Engine
Search for this:
mars
Submit
Options
Webinator Help
Heritage Home
Hubble Heritage Search

The main search providers will help to locate relevant sites in the first place. Try some of the following to identify the best one for you:

- www.google.co.uk – good advanced search; simple, effective and fast; with filtering tools
- www.ask.co.uk – simple, effective and fast

- http://yahooligans.yahoo.com/reference/ – child friendly; simple but commercial
- http://vivisimo.com/ – clusters results into subgroups, which can be useful
- http://www.lycos.com/ – some advanced search tools; with filtering tools
- www.bbc.co.uk – family friendly; UK focused

Once you have chosen a search engine, the keyword or words can be entered. Sometimes you will encounter a reference to 'Boolean' operators. Based on the logical system of symbols developed by George Boole, the nineteenth-century English mathematician, they describe the way that searches can be extended or narrowed down. Take, for example, two keywords 'primary' and 'science'; searching for primary **or** science will produce a wide search which returns pages with either term. Searching for primary **and** science will only return those pages which have both words somewhere in the text. If, however, I search for pages that contain 'primary science' as an exact phrase, then those medical pages which talk about *primary health care* and mention *science* somewhere else will be excluded. Another Boolean term is **not**, which is useful to narrow down a search by excluding pages that include a particular word. For instance, when searching for information concerning animals which have been adopted by sporting teams, if 'sharks' is one of your keywords, then specifying **not** 'rugby' will remove pages about the Sale Sharks rugby team.

Those search engines with advanced search options enable the selection of words or phrases and the exclusion of other terms to be chosen as an advanced search by filling in a form like the one below.

Google **Advanced Search** Advanced Search Tips |

Find results	with **all** of the words	10 results · Google Search
	with the **exact phrase**	
	with **at least one** of the words	
	without the words	
Language	Return pages written in	any language
File Format	Only · return results of the file format	any format
Date	Return web pages updated in the	anytime
Occurrences	Return results where my terms occur	anywhere in the page
Domain	Only · return results from the site or domain	e.g. google.com, .org More info
SafeSearch	⦿ No filtering ○ Filter using SafeSearch	

Restrictions to the format, provenance, date or language of pages returned in the search can also be made. If you only want pages from UK universities, for example, then choosing **.ac.uk** as the domain will filter out any other pages.

Many search engines without advanced features will also respond to the following conventions:

" " To conduct a search for an exact phrase, use quotation marks around it, e.g. "primary science"

\+ Use a plus sign for words that MUST be included in the results, e.g. primary+science

– Use a minus sign for words that MUST NOT be included in the results, e.g. primary+science–healthcare

How to store web page locations in **Favorites** (*sic*)

Internet Explorer has a **Favorites** menu which enables the address (URL) of the web page that you are currently viewing to be saved. Netscape refer to this process as 'bookmarking' and you are effectively marking the corner of the page so that you can return to it quickly. Depending on the set-up of your computer network you may find that the Favorites list is saved to the computer, meaning that children need to return to the same machine to access their saved pages.

Organising Favorites

It is possible to create sub-folders in the **Favorites** menu which helps to organise the pages that have been saved. The folder can either be created for the children to use or they could be shown how to make their own. First select **Organize Favorites . . .** from the **Favorites** menu.

In the dialogue box that opens, folders can be created or renamed, and saved Favorites can be moved, renamed or deleted.

Create a new folder by clicking on the **Create Folder** button and typing a name for the project or the group.

Click and drag existing individual Favorites to your folder or select each Favorite and click **Move to Folder . . .**

If you wish to create additional folders to structure your Favorites, then the process is the same. When you have finished you can click on the **Favorites** menu and check the contents of your folders.

Once you have located a page that you wish to visit again, you need to add it to your new folder in **Favorites**. With the web page displayed in the browser window select **Add to Favorites . . .** from the **Favorites** menu. The **Add Favorite** window will appear. Make sure that you select the correct folder to save your page in and click **OK**. It is possible to create new folders at this stage by clicking on **New Folder . . .** and naming it.

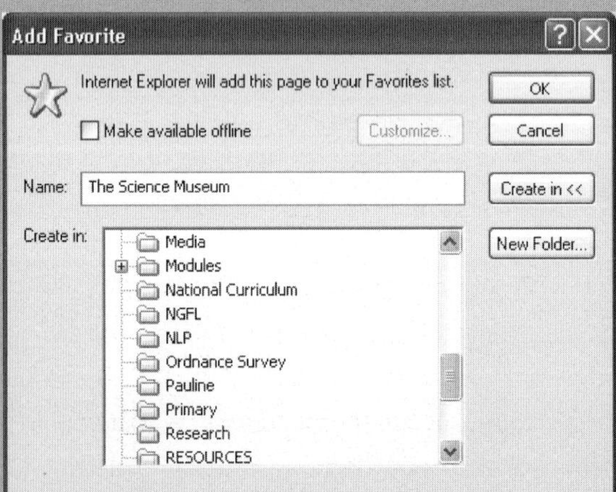

Check that the page you have added is actually in the **Favorites** by selecting the **Favorites** menu again. You should see the page which you have just viewed added to the folder that you specified.

You can continue searching and browsing for pages and build up a collection of Favorites.

How to copy text from a web page

Once a collection of web pages relating to the topic has been identified, elements from those pages can be copied and pasted into the software being used to create the book or presentation. An electronic form of note taking can be taught to the children by copying a section from a web page, pasting it and then deleting everything apart from the key facts; the children can then weave those key notes into their own writing, considering the needs of the audience. To take an extract of text from a web page, first click and drag across the text that you require to highlight it. You may find that you need several attempts to get the right piece of text because of the page formatting. It is also necessary to move the mouse smartly as you click and avoid clicking on hyperlinks.

> Tip:
> Text can be selected by clicking once at the beginning, holding down **SHIFT** and clicking again at the end.

Sound is a form of energy. The more energy produced in one place, the greater effect that energy will have in another if it is allowed to get there.

Example:- Throw a stone = Energy expelled

Get hit by a stone = Energy received !!

The harder the stone is thrown, the more it hurts !

There are three ways of stopping the stone hurting. **1:-** Wear something very dense, the stone will bounce off. You may feel the dent where it hit, but its effect will be reduced. **2:-** Wear something very thick and soft, the power of the stone will be absorbed by the softness. You may still feel the stone, but the force will be greatly reduced. **3:-** Get to the joker with the stone.

Once you have the required text selected choose **Copy** from the **Edit** menu, or use the **Ctrl+C** shortcut.

Inserting your text in a *Word* document

Open the *Word* document that you wish to insert the text into, click where you would like the text to be and then select **Edit** > **Paste,** or use **Ctrl+V.**

Sometimes you will find that tables and formatting from the web page will also be pasted into your document. If the formatting is not required and the text is all that you want, then select **Paste Special . . .** from the **Edit** menu instead and choose **Unformatted Text.**

How to copy images from a web page

Copying images

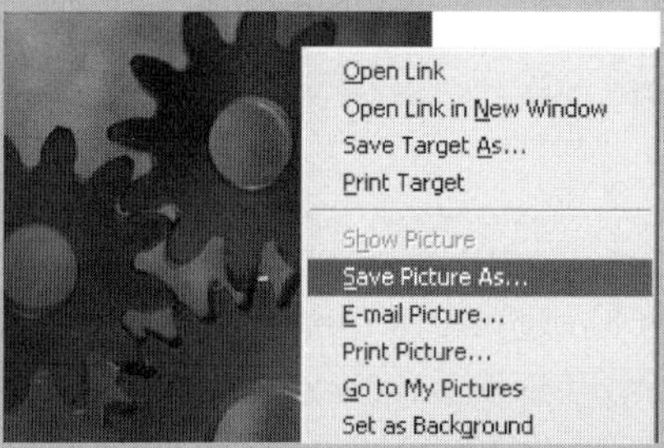

Once you have the web page containing the image that you require on the screen, clicking on it with the right mouse button will produce a menu which includes the **Save Picture As . . .** option. Select **Save Picture As . . .** and select where you wish to save it.

Inserting your image in a *Word* document (or other word processor/ DTP package)

Open the document that you wish to insert the image into, click where you would like the image to be and then select **Insert** > **Picture** > **From File . . .**

Navigate to the folder where the image was saved and select it and click **OK**. You can position, resize and crop the image in the document; in *Word* and *PowerPoint* more advanced facilities are available using the **Picture** toolbar.

To bring up the **Picture** toolbar select **View** > **Toolbars** > **Picture.**

It is also possible to use copy and paste with images, but saving the images to your computer makes it possible to open the files in a picture editor and alter them.

What will the children learn?

The children will learn how information in electronic format can be shared and manipulated as well as benefiting from reading and interpreting scientific information.

That information can be presented in a variety of forms and collected from a variety of sources

The variety of types of information can be shown through demonstration and by setting expectations for the children's topic books to contain a defined minimum range of types and sources.

To use appropriate search techniques to find information

Challenge children to locate specific types or pieces of information. It is usually possible to search within results and so narrow a search further or suggest that they change their keywords or technique using AND + OR " " NOT.

That information can be connected in different ways at the same time

Where several keywords identify information, searches can make connections between different types of information and quite different searches can produce the same item of information.

To use the tools in online search engines to find out the answers to specific questions

Setting closed questions to locate key facts can be turned into timed treasure hunts or WebQuests (for more information on WebQuests developed by Bernie Dodge at San Diego State University, see http://webquest.sdsu.edu/ or http://www.ozline.com/learning/). See also English Project 10 – Macbeth Webquest.

That searches can be carried out using more than one criterion

Some work with Venn diagrams can help children to see how careful search criteria can narrow down a set and thereby gain access to information more quickly.

To use complex searches to locate information

Using the advance search features described above will demonstrate how careful construction of a search avoids having to sift through too many results.

To understand the importance of choosing keywords to find information

Helping the children to select those keywords which are likely to appear on related pages only is an increasingly important skill. (In fact, there is a whole website devoted to the art of devising pairs of keywords that return only one web page known as 'Googlewhacking' – see http://www.googlewhack.com/ for a bit of harmless fun.)

Challenging the more able and supporting the less able: modifying the project for older and younger pupils

There are many websites which provide plenty of information about specific topics, so some children can be supported by restricting their search to a single site's search engine. For others, providing them with a document containing a series of links to specific sites for them to use as a 'launch pad' can ensure success. A type of 'treasure hunt' template for their topic, with a finite number of pieces of information required, can also scaffold less experienced children; clues or links to specific sites will make their searching less frustrating.

More experienced children can be challenged to find specific pieces of information in a wider range of formats – like a video of astronauts playing football with a moon rock! As a teacher using the internet, do not expect to know all that is available; if you acknowledge when children have found new resources and information, it is a powerful motivation for them to learn.

Other children can be encouraged to focus on the interpretation and repurposing of the information that they have gathered in order for their scientific, linguistic and ICT capabilities to be challenged and developed. It is important to recognise that there is a huge quantity of unchecked and inaccurate information published on the internet; anybody can – and many do – create their own website. It is important that we all check the source and plausibility of information. Help the children to read URLs: information from www.bbc.co.uk is likely to have been checked; similarly, URLs which contain **.edu** (US education) or **.ac** (UK academic) should be reliable.

Why teach this?

Focusing on section 1 of the ICT NC KS2 PoS, 'Finding things out', this project provides an opportunity to highlight the benefits of obtaining and communicating information using ICT in an integrated and purposeful way. It helps the children learn to develop their ideas in either a processed and printed document or presentation described in statement 2a. Using either *PowerPoint* or word-processing software can help thoughts and ideas to be developed and clarified. The final purpose of sharing the information with their peers or younger children or parents can be used to address statements 3a and 3b of the PoS. While the opportunity to discuss the strengths and weaknesses of the use of ICT for this type of searching as required by the 'Reviewing, modifying and evaluating work as it progresses' strand of the ICT PoS is possible, it will not happen unless specific time for reflection is planned.

The project builds on the content of QCA ICT Scheme of Work Unit 3C: *Introduction to databases*, as the internet, while not structured like a database, can be searched in a similar way. The expectation that the information gathered will be shared can be used to address or build on Unit 4A: *Writing for different audiences.* The key purposes of Units 5B: *Analysing data and asking questions: using complex searches* and 5C: *Evaluating information, checking accuracy and questioning plausibility* can also be incorporated in this project. The activities involved provide a scientific context for Unit 6D: *Using the internet to search large databases and to interpret information.*

As primarily a research activity this project will need to be complemented by other Sc1 activities related to the area of learning. Depending on the topic, the activity can contribute to children's knowledge and understanding in Sc2, researching plants or animals, Sc3, researching materials, or Sc4, finding out about the solar system. Sc1, 2h will be addressed through the use of ICT to communicate appropriately. The use of the internet in this way to support teaching and learning can enhance and extend the QCA Science scheme of work units such as 5E: *Earth, Sun and Moon*, 5D: *Changing state* or 5F: *Changing sounds.*

See also *Humanities* Project 3 (*Using an information source*), *Humanities* Project 5 (*Repurposing information for different audiences*), *Humanities* Project 8 (*Making an information source*) and *English* Project 10 (*A Macbeth webquest*) for related activities.

Index